The Space Between Us

The Space Between Us

AWAKENING TOGETHER
IN A FRACTURED WORLD

PETER MITCHELL

EMERGENCE EDUCATION
Philadelphia, Pennsylvania

Copyright © 2025 by Peter Mitchell

All rights reserved. Except as permitted under U.S. Copyright Act of 1976, no part of this publication may be reproduced, distributed, or transmitted in any form or by any means, or stored in a database or retrieval system, without the prior written permission of the publisher.

ISBN: 978-1-954642-72-0

Emergence Education Press
P.O. Box 63767
Philadelphia, PA 19147
emergenceeducation.com

Cover design concept by Peter Mitchell
Cover image: "Digital Neural Web" by StockCake (Public Domain)
Interior design by Sophie Peirce

Printed in the United States of America

*This book is a sonata in three movements—
an invitation to listen, feel, and respond to
the living rhythm of awakening between us.*

*It is not a solo aria, but a composition with choral
passages, where many voices contribute to an
emerging harmony, rich with counterpoint—
each voice distinct yet woven into a greater whole.*

*The three movements will take you on a journey
from first recognition,
through deeper exploration
to emergent possibility.*

*Each contains three motifs, like musical phrases
that build upon one another,
creating a composition that invites you
to not just witness but participate in its unfolding.*

"The grace that is being given at this time is not interested in personal development. It is not concerned with individual well-being. Its purpose is to open up the energy channels that exist within our collective psyche and collective consciousness and help the heart of the world awaken. We have become so focussed on ourselves we have forgotten what has always been true, that the world itself has a higher nature, and that we are part of this greater reality."

— Llewellyn Vaughan-Lee

Contents

Dedication xi

A Foretone: by Anne Sweet
A Whisper Before the First Note xiii

Prelude:
An Invitation to You xv

Overture:
An Emerging Field of Consciousness xix

**First Movement – Discovering the Living Field –
The Silence begins to Speak** 1

Motif 1: A Spark Ignites –
How the Field Came Alive 3

Motif 2: The Flame Quickens –
Finding Our Feet as a Group 21

Motif 3: The Fire Spreads –
The Courage to Expand 33

**Second Movement – Digging Deeper –
Finding the Context** 49

Motif 4: The Mystery Between Us –
Awakening as Relationship 53

Motif 5: Your Path is the Portal –
Authenticity is the Key to the Kingdom 61

Motif 6: The Roots of Separation –
Dropping the Masks of Otherness 73

Third Movement – The Far Horizon – Seeding the New 89

   Motif 7: The Emergent Field –
   Coherence, a Living Mystery... 93

   Motif 8: A New Way of Awakening –
   Resonance as Transmission 103

   Motif 9: The Future of Interbeing –
   A Fractal Emergence... 117

Coda 135

Harmonics of Meaning
A Glossary of Terms and Resonances 141

Field Notes & Jazz Variations
Appendices 145

   Appendix I: Glimpses from the Future........................ 149

   Appendix II: Resonant Echoes 152

   Appendix III: Living Patterns....................................... 160

   Appendix IV: Distilled Wisdom................................... 168

Acknowledgements 173

About the Author 177

Dedication

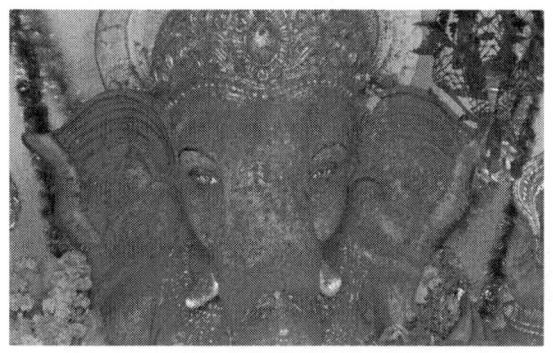

For **Lord Ganesha**,
who catalysed my spiritual exploration
during a flight to Kathmandu in 1993

A Foretone: by Anne Sweet

A Whisper Before the First Note

In the early months of the group's emergence, **Anne**, one of the original four members wrote this vision. At the time, it felt idealistic—aspirational. But as our experience of the field has deepened and matured, this vision begins to feel less like a distant hope and more like a quiet remembering.

It serves here as a foretone, like a musical theme sensed before the first notes are played.

—

11 November 2022

> **In my ideal world ...**
>
> ... one way of passing on the perennial wisdom without the inherent power imbalances and often ugly distortions of the usual teacher/student relationship would be for a small group of self-realized/spiritually mature people operating as a self-regulating collective to come together, whose sole purpose was the spiritual/human development of self and others.

The group members would be acting from a 'higher calling' and not needing to promote a personal agenda or ideology or being seen as the teacher or 'knower'. The group will have already established between themselves a rare degree of trust, intimacy and true spiritual union – a unified field of love, authenticity and non-separation.

Together they would provide an open forum for spiritual seekers to ask questions and receive responses based on the collective wisdom of the group, including that of the questioners. With a foundation of no fixed dogma or personal 'knower' to protect and uphold, the responses emerge from the spacious, unknowing ground of true collective interpersonal wisdom. This collective ground or field is the crucible for the evolution of the individual (and the group) – a safe, sacred, dynamic and infinitely creative space free from the usual fixations on an individual teacher and their specific worldview and approach.

Prelude:
An Invitation to You

There are moments in life when something shifts so profoundly that the world is never the same again. Not because we have learned something new, but because we have seen with fresh eyes. This book is about one such shift—one that does not belong to any single individual but arises *between* us, in the shared space of being-together.

For much of my spiritual journey, I sought awakening as something personal—a deepening of insight, a loosening of identity, a realization into the vast openness of awareness. And yet, it eventually dawned on me, that my most profound moments of transformation did not happen in solitude but in connection. It was in meeting others *beyond* the usual constructs of self and other that something truly new emerged.

This discovery—of a shared, inter-personal awakening—changed everything. It was not about one enlightened person leading the way, nor about merging into a collective identity. Instead, it was about the space we meet in – *the space* between *us* – coming alive. A field of awareness, presence, and intelligence that is both deeply personal and entirely transpersonal. A space where we meet beyond the limitations of the conditioned mind, not as isolated individuals but as a dynamic, emergent whole.

The tension between autonomy and belonging is one of the core dilemmas of our fractured time. Some give themselves entirely to movements or ideologies: others retreat into personal spiritual quests, seeking transcendence and refuge. But what if there is another way?

What if the very thing that seems to divide—our individuality—could become the bridge to a deeper, more unified way of being together, and of being in the world? What if we could engage without losing ourselves, belong without conforming, and discover an intimacy that doesn't require compromise?

This book invites that exploration. It weaves personal experience with historical and contemporary context: poetic insight, developmental maps like Spiral Dynamics and Integral Theory, and real-world examples—Quaker meetings, Parker Palmer's Circles of Trust, Otto Scharmer's Theory U…

This isn't merely an intellectual exploration. It is a call to *participation*. The awakening explored within these pages is not something one person can achieve alone. It is something we create together—through listening, openness and the willingness to meet one another beyond our habitual patterns.

Some reading these words may arrive after years of formal practice; others by a thread of intuition or longing. It is not my role to decide who is ready. My task in writing this book is simply to keep the space clear and faithful to what wants to be shared.

As you turn these pages, I invite you to sense what's possible beneath the surface of these words. The space between us is not a metaphor—it's alive, waiting to be recognised. Let's explore it—together.

Overture:
An Emerging Field of Consciousness

A gentle note before we begin.

Every so often in human history, something new begins to stir—not just in individuals, but in many places at once. A shift in how we relate, how we understand ourselves, and how we come together. Often it starts quietly —on the edge of things. No fanfare, no big announcements. Just a sense that something is changing.

I believe something like that is happening now.

Across the world, small groups are meeting in new ways—without formal structures, gurus, or rigid ideologies. They're drawn by a quiet longing to reconnect: with each other, with presence, and with something larger than themselves.

In these times of isolation, fragmentation, and hyper-individualism, such gatherings offer more than a sanctuary. They are chambers of transformation—not just for individuals but for how we relate to life itself. Perhaps even for culture itself.

These spaces may look different on the surface, but there's a common thread—a subtle sense that something essential is being uncovered, together.

This book tells the story of one such group. It's not a blueprint, not a model, but a lived account of what unfolded when a few of us followed a thread of connection that led somewhere unexpected.

We've come to realise we are not alone in this. Far from it. Many others are sensing the same possibility. It seems to be arising organically—a convergent evolution nudging us towards a new way of being.

What follows in the First Movement is how this began for us. How a chance meeting of four friends grew into something larger. A field of awareness and connection that continues to unfold and surprise us.

This isn't a metaphor, but a lived experience—a presence that appears when we meet in openness and authenticity. That subtle yet unmistakable shift when conversation deepens into a shared space of meaning.

Maybe this is the future of spiritual transmission—not from teacher to student but through mutual presence. The space between us is not just container, but catalyst—alive with the possibility of shared transformation. This may even be an early crest of the next wave of evolution for the human species itself.

We share it in the spirit of participation—not as experts, not as authorities, but as fellow travellers who've found something worth tending and sharing.

Let's begin.

First Movement – Discovering the Living Field –

The Silence begins to Speak

*"There is no such thing as an isolated thing.
Everything is what it is only in relation to something else."*

— Iain McGilchrist.
Author of '*The Matter with Things*'

THE PARTY

Last night, I went to a party.
Everyone there was a friend—
and more than a friend.

We all wore our best attire,
and admired how beautiful we all looked.

Then one person had the nerve
to reveal she was completely naked!

In that moment,
we realised our garments were see-through—
there was nowhere left to hide.

And in our complete transparency,
we dissolved
into a sustained, infinite moment—
beyond time, beyond space, beyond concept.

Motif 1:
A Spark Ignites –

How the Field Came Alive

*"The space between us is not empty.
It is alive with potential."*

— Inspired by Martin Buber and Emergence Theory

KINDLING

We meet in the Silence.
We drop our barriers
and lower the protections
of our fragile, imagined selves,
and hand in hand we wade out
through the shallows of intimacy,
until we are swimming together
in the endless depths of pure Being—
with currents of Love and Joy
and deep Peace flowing
in and around us.

Just below the surface,
a passion is bubbling forth,
longing to be discovered and expressed.

At one with shared Presence—
that has no name,
but is the source of All—
we come together.
Yet it is not for us alone.
This depth that calls to us
wants more:
for it is the universal,
carrying and connecting everything,
and it is pulling us to share
its wonder, beauty, and trust.

The flame that sprang into being
with the four of us at the start
sparked a fire that now burns between us.
But we few are just kindling—
ready to ignite a conflagration
that wants to grow, to attract
ever more into its loving embrace,
until we are consumed
by our own Self:
as the unmanifest, infinite potential
seeks to bring something unimaginable
into manifestation—
in this dark and challenging world.

An Unlikely Beginning

In late 2022, four friends—with a shared history of seeking spiritual realisation in an intense spiritual community—met on Zoom with no agenda other than to reconnect.

It had been many years since we had been together in the same organisation, and we knew each other with varying degrees of intimacy. One of us had had an awakening since leaving that community and had recently emerged as a fresh new voice in the spiritual world.

Although we weren't aware of it at the time, she had received a strong intuition to convene a meeting between the four of us and carried a sense of responsibility for making it happen, without knowing why—just that it had to happen.

What unfolded between us during that call was spacious, easeful, enjoyable and quietly luminous. Nothing dramatic occurred, and yet we all felt nourished. It was unusual to experience such lightness, fearlessness and freedom in spiritual company.

Something precious had quietly begun.

The Realisation Afterward

But it wasn't until the day afterwards, in the stillness that lingered, that we began to recognise that something interesting and unexpected had happened between us.

Each of us, in our own way, was aware of something awakening—not just between us, but within us too. It was like a tuning fork had been struck in the meeting space and continued resonating in each of us long after the call had ended.

In our meeting, there was an undercurrent of intimacy that was immediate and open, independent of our shared history and much more interested in what connected us right now. It was like seeing each other with fresh eyes and recognising something in each of us that had nothing to do with what we already knew.

That resonance gave us our first glimpse: something precious had sparked. A subtle, unnameable presence had woven itself into our awareness.

We knew we wanted to meet again.

The Fire Between Us

At first, we met as often as our schedules allowed, guided more by spontaneity than structure.

There was no pressure, just a simple delight in meeting in this way. Each time we met, it was as if we sank a little deeper, like slowly wading out into the ocean.

> *"Sometimes we would fall into silence, not the uncomfortable awkward silences when no-one has anything to say but aware that the silence was a presence joining us.*

Sometimes there would be joy, light humour and playfulness as we became willing to drop our defences and enjoy each other's presence. At other times we would fall naturally into a meditative space." PM

Each meeting was different, with its own energy—sometimes bubbling joy, sometimes deep meditative stillness, sometimes a shared recognition that what we were part of was extraordinary.

There was no pressure to do anything with it other than enjoy it.

We simply relished the freshness of being together in a way we hadn't known before.

Gratitude naturally arose. Trust quietly deepened. We began to feel held by something larger than ourselves, maybe a subtle field of being, and something we didn't need to name or define.

Catalysts and Starting Conditions

In any alchemical experiment, the starting conditions are crucial to the outcome. So it seems important to offer some background—how the four of us first came to meet, and the kind of spiritual exposure that shaped the context for our shared communal lives.

By the time we reconnected in 2022, the spiritual community where we had originally met had long since dissolved in turmoil. Yet during the years of immersion within its ethos, we were trained—often rigorously—in the art of group dialogue. This training emphasised not simply speaking, but listening, attuning, and following a thread of inquiry together, rather than waiting to insert a carefully prepared opinion. Over time, this fostered a sensitivity to the authentic voice—an instinctive attunement capable of discerning when someone spoke from genuine presence. Anything less would often ring hollow under the group's unsparing scrutiny.

But there were two sides to the experience. While this training left us with deep discernment, many of us also found those meetings difficult to join in. The pressure to speak from a certain level of clarity—or to perform a kind of sanctioned authenticity—meant that anything less was met with intense challenge. Not being seen to "rise" was interpreted as failure—or worse, wilful intransigence—and could lead to painful scrutiny or even public shaming.

Looking back, what was described as compassion often landed as coercion. The teachings, though profound in parts, had become increasingly disconnected from the human context in which they were being applied. Those of us from that background have long known the not-so-subtle wall of fear we had to face whenever we wanted to speak in a group context—an internal hesitation that lingered long after the community dissolved.

That's what surprised us most in those early meetings of the original four: we met immediately in a deep trust that allowed an intimacy none of us expected.

The teacher of that former community had envisioned a collective enlightenment—a "new being" arising from individuals meeting beyond identity. But the high-pressure conditions and confrontational style that permeated the environment were, in retrospect, antithetical to the kind of spaciousness and trust we would later discover were essential for intimacy to take root.

In my experience, the radical intimacy, radiant transparency, and deep trust needed to ignite the emergence of a shared field were rare during those years. When such experiences did occur, they were usually outside the spotlight of the teacher's unrelenting gaze—quiet moments of connection that evaded the dominant structure.

By the time we came together again, each of us had spent far more time outside that community than within it. And there was no sense of attempting to recreate what had gone before. Still, perhaps the seeds were planted in those earlier days—and in the fertile soil of mutual respect and unforced intimacy, something unexpected and deeply welcome began to flower.

The Invitation to Others

Over time, the rhythm began to shift.

A quiet questioning began to surface in some of us.

> *Is this beautiful space just for us?*
> *What about inviting other friends with a similar history to join with us and share in the extraordinary intimacy?*

Some of us were curious to see whether this shared presence could include others and remain intact. Others were slightly more hesitant, feeling it might disturb the trust that was growing.

Tentatively and after much discussion we decided to each invite one or two people—those who we felt might be attuned to what was unfolding.

Nurturing the Tender Beginnings

As the group slowly expanded, a gentle structure needed to take shape. Coordinating diaries across countries became ever more complex, and spontaneity gave way to rhythm. We began meeting every three weeks on a set day and time, making it easier for everyone to plan ahead and remain connected.

Alongside the larger gatherings every three weeks, the original four of us continued to meet in between—to reflect on how things were unfolding, consider what adjustments might be needed, discuss who to invite next, and gently tend what still felt tender and fragile.

We also stayed closely in touch via a chat app, sharing insights, questions, and impressions. We knew we were curating something precious—something not yet ready to stand entirely on its own, even as we could feel it quietly gaining strength with each meeting.

> *"Hi Guys, In meditation this morning, I had a very strong image of a beautiful circle of light threading*

> *through all nine of the souls who are currently part of our expanding group and I could sense all of us as part of its current flowing around and through us"* PM

There was something quietly alive in the space between us, something not of our making but clearly responsive to how we showed up. A growing recognition emerged: a subtle presence—relational, intelligent, and alive—that seemed to hold and shape our encounters. Over time we sensed this as a subtle *field of being*.

When the Meetings Wobbled

As new voices and energies joined us over the next few months, our meetings grew more diverse in flavour—brighter at times, but also bumpier.

More faces meant more perspectives—and with them, more divergent opinions about how the meetings were unfolding and even why we were meeting at all. New members would often arrive carrying the weight of their identities—their expertise, histories, or frameworks—not yet having experienced the gradual shedding of these layers that had allowed the original group to access the field more directly. At times this created a tangible shift in the quality of our gatherings.

There was often a nervousness at the start, a hesitancy to open up. We tended to stay in safer, more familiar waters, waiting for someone to take the lead and dive deeper. Sometimes, the space would fill with monologues rather than dialogue—statements that seemed to close down rather than open up our exploration.

The space between us didn't fall apart, though it occasionally trembled. What we had begun to sense as a subtle field of being could lose coherence, especially when personal stories or emotional reactivity began to dominate. It was as if the shared presence we were learning to trust had become fainter—still there, but harder to feel. It became clear that the quality of the field itself depended on our ability to notice these shifts, to take the risk to speak from presence, and so gently redirect when the personal began to colour the transpersonal.

Our practice had been to allow each voice space, to follow rather than interrupt the natural flow of conversation. Yet there were moments when this approach itself became an obstacle to the deeper connection we were cultivating. This sometimes required difficult interventions—moments when the usual pattern of allowing each thread to unfold completely had to be gently but firmly redirected.

> *It took one of us—with the most experience and the deepest sensitivity to the field—to take the lead, and anchor and steady it. PM*

They offered a guiding hand, as someone more familiar with the territory, willing to stand against the inertia of group mind and providing a focal point of clarity in confusion. These redirections weren't about controlling content but rather about reorienting the group back toward presence rather than performance, toward listening rather than declaring.

These interventions weren't always immediately welcomed and were sometimes met with resistance. The usually open sense of presence could feel contracted, and I too felt the pull to retreat behind personal barriers—to escape the confusion, disruption, and agitation. Suddenly, not knowing how to respond became a problem, rather than an open door to freedom. The fact that one of us had taken the risk to stand up helped steady us all. Still, feathers had been ruffled, and a few people left during this period—perhaps feeling that the space wasn't what they had expected or needed.

Yet there was also a growing sensitivity within the group to the unfiltered voice of those expressing vulnerability. It was this that supported and celebrated the energies drawing us back to the real intimacy of the moment—and helped nurture the unfolding as it happened.

Gradually, we learned how to respond in ways that cultivated, rather than drained, the field. Some of us who had been part of the group since its early days began to take more responsibility for sustaining a sense of presence in our meetings. And in turn, as we made ourselves available to the field, it seemed to nourish us—quietly strengthening our capacity to hold space, listen more deeply, and trust the deeper current that moved through us all.

But that's jumping ahead.

Something Larger Was Holding Us

We began to sense the coherence more clearly, and something remarkable came into focus. We noticed that when someone relaxed into the shared space—even after being caught in heaviness—they would shift.

What had seemed like a problem dissolved. The person became buoyant, clear, even joyful. It wasn't about fixing anything. It was about returning to the presence that was always there, just beneath the surface.

A growing sense that this wasn't just "our" space began to arise in our conversations. It had its own intelligence, its own rhythm.

> *It felt like the space was alive—*
> *not just something we entered,*
> *but something that also entered us.*

The relational field we were meeting in was opening an inner space in each of us—enabling us to listen more deeply, to step aside from our usual selves, and to start to trust something emergent. The spaciousness we experienced in the meetings began to mirror itself within us, revealing an inner clarity we hadn't known we were capable of. It was as if a quiet part of ourselves, long hidden and protected beneath roles and reactions, was being invited to step forward and take its place.

And although we only met every few weeks, we sensed we had joined one long conversation with no beginning or end that was unfolding through us and as us, and yet independent of who might turn up on any one occasion.

An Early Discovery

When someone spoke from a place of vulnerability or insight, the field itself would become more apparent. The stillness deepened. Everyone was more present. The deep listening became almost palpable.

At times, we might fall into spontaneous sustained silence—a meditation—not awkward but vibrant.

We learned not to fill silences too quickly.

> *As the extraordinary nature of what we were uncovering became ever more apparent…something in us relaxed.*

A lightness of being would arise between us—bubbling into shared giggles, warm humour and quiet awe at of what we were uncovering together.

Sensing a way ahead – just out of reach

From the earliest days, there was an unmistakable sense that something rare and precious was revealing itself between us. Though undefined, it was a shared glimpse into a larger unfolding. As one of us wrote at the time:

> *"…Can you get a glimpse of where this is going? I have a little glimpse. It is the most precious thing because it does not belong to any one of us – it is a gift that is being given to us to share"* AS

Another replied:

> *"Yes, I do have a glimpse – it's just out of reach around the corner, just across the road pulling us all forward into the unknown, tantalisingly glorious and always moving us forward to rediscover it – it has no fixed form or obvious direction other than wherever it wants to explore...."* PM

And later:

> *"....I think we all recognised the potential inherent in our meetings from the very beginning without having any concept of what that might look like – just a deep positive feeling that it wanted to include more hearts in its embrace. ......an international enlightened mind combined with a growing international heart that wraps its embrace around our planet. The combination of heart and mind made up of multiple souls may start to impact the momentum of the world in some undefinable way. It's wonderful to share that love with you all."* PM

These glimpses became a gentle thread between meetings, pulling us forward—teasing us with possibilities we couldn't yet imagine.

What is this Field?

Although we often commented on the sense of a deeper presence between us—greater intimacy, gentle trust and more space for the complexity of being human—we never attempted to analyse it.

It was the ocean lifting us
The air we breathed together.
The undercurrent of everything unfolding.

So, what is this field of being?

In writing this book, that was the first question I had to sit with.

Not to define it,

Not to catch it—*that would be like trying to catch a river in a bucke*t.

But to recognise:

When we meet and relax our barriers, our boundaries, when we loosen our sense of identity, something extraordinary emerges. The experience is of sharing a real and palpable intimacy, something beyond words that cannot be defined, only recognised. When someone speaks, it touches us more deeply than at the mere intellectual level—it resonates in our sense of self as true, as insightful, as authentic and relatable.

We become aware of a shared presence, a heightened sense of listening that carries a level of intensity, of concentration, yet remains relaxed, not forced. We can see just by looking that we are immersed in a similar joint experience—people 'light up,' their eyes sparkle. The sense of exploring at the edge of the known rather than merely repeating brings an aliveness to the space, a sense of anticipation without expectation.

It's not something external, magical or other, that happens to us.
It's who we are—in the space between us

It's an awareness of the organic connection we share—deeper than the surface-level ways we usually relate. We recognise it as the presence already here, revealed when our limited sense of self recedes into the background. And our meetings offer the perfect space for that shift to occur

Are we sinking together into a more foundational layer of being where the boundaries between self and other are more permeable, or even non-existent?

In these moments of intersubjective coherence, are we touching Universal Mind?

Could the underlying unity of the universe be becoming perceptible through individuals being together?

These are questions to be held lightly. They invite a sense of wonder and curiosity, and are not intended to have concrete answers, they simply open our eyes to a living vital thread that becomes more visible when we discover it in the space between us.

Reflection: Tending the Fire

That early spark showed us something important: the light we found between us wasn't separate from the light within us. And meeting in that space—without an agenda, without needing to know—has a way of catching fire.

The kindling is our presence, our honesty, our willingness to show up without defence. And once it starts burning, it can light the way ahead—not just for us, but for something far larger than we imagined.

If you have a group of friends or kindred spirits, consider this:

> What might happen if you gathered not to discuss or debate but to listen—not just to each other, but to the space between you?

> What qualities would help keep that space open, curious, and alive?

> What would it take to tend that fire together?

Motif 2:
The Flame Quickens –

Finding Our Feet as a Group

"Out beyond ideas of wrongdoing and rightdoing,
There is a field. I'll meet you there.
When the soul lies down in that grass,
The world is too full to talk about.
Ideas, language, even the phrase each other
Doesn't make any sense."

—Rumi, translated by Coleman Barks
in *The Essential Rumi*

INHERENT MAGIC

Beyond the usual boundaries of the separate little me,
we meet—beyond time, beyond place.
A motley crew of seekers who have become finders,
with a shared purpose: to express, together,
the truth of who we are.

Yet:
The Zoom grid shows us as little boxes—
eager, sometimes nervous faces
lit up in anticipation
of what the coming minutes will reveal and unfold.

We believe we are separate individuals turning up,
fingers crossed that the magic will appear—
the magic of disappearing
into one field of attention.

We treat it as special.
Each of us carries the burden of making it happen,
and the fear that it might slip away
under the pressure of the clock.

But the truth is different.
That unified field of non-separate awareness
is who we already are—period!
It is our real identity (if such a thing even exists),
long before we join the meeting.

How would it be
if we all showed up

with nothing but our Original Faces—
taking it as a given, not casually,
but without hesitant expectation,
that the magic is inherent in being together?

Then we could dance and play in unconstrained awareness,
untethered to anything fixed or known.
The ever-new moment—a stream to swim and splash in,
joyous play in deep trust
and heartfelt communion.

A Settling In

As the group continued to meet, something began to deepen.

There was a gentle acknowledgement of the trust between us. The nervousness we would sometimes experience at the start of a meeting shifted to a quiet sense of anticipation at where this meeting might transport us.

We had weathered a few choppy meetings and began to sense a shared capacity growing among the regulars. A subtler current started to emerge—meetings flowed more easily, people opened more gently, and there was a natural sense of inner confidence to be present without the need to already know where we were going.

The meetings became an open invitation to participate and there was room for everything from light banter to profound reflective moments. We began to swim together in deeper, more stable waters.

An Open Invitation to Explore

It is as if each meeting starts with a question mark.

We meet in an open space of enquiry, not for personal grandstanding.

There is a tingling curiosity and wonder at how the meeting will unfold and what aspect of our human potential will be uncovered. We meet at the edge of our understanding, pulling on threads that lead us beyond what we already know.

Each of us is a unique crucible, a living experiment in which we dissect and take apart those deeper aspects of our common humanity to uncover what it means to live simply in presence.

Together we unravel the unconscious mechanisms that keep us stuck in the maze of the grasping mind. We share our inner discoveries so all can experience those moments of gentle revelation, and we follow someone into the thrill of uncovering something they never realised they already knew—beyond knowing.

In these shared moments, a different kind of learning occurs—not the acquisition of knowledge, but the awakening of a new way of sensing. It's as if we are growing another way of seeing, a deeper capacity to meet life as it is, together.

A Deepening Respect

There is never any pressure to attend every meeting—people come when they can.

Those who show up regularly, are developing an intuitive fluency and steadying presence within the shared field. The responsibility for maintaining the integrity of the space no longer relies on just one person but is being shared between those finding their own feet in the unknown.

Humble Authority

They help to hold the space gracefully if turbulence arises, and they exude a natural authority—simple, grounded, and clear. There is no need to prove or persuade. Just being centred in themselves allows others to do the same.

It isn't just trust in the shared space but also the awakening of a quiet confidence in ourselves

> *"... whoever takes the lead in any one moment takes the whole group with them into a deeper, totally shared perspective. There is a resonant mutuality that is of a different order to normal spiritual transmission...."*

What emerges is a humble, natural authority rooted in the presence between us. It isn't about dominating or leading others. It is a grounded awareness that comes from being fully present and transparent. No-one imposes anything; they simply inhabit their own clarity, and that gives others permission to do the same.

A Foundation for Change

Many of us experienced these meetings as a catalyst for personal growth—not through acquiring something new, but by uncovering a quiet inner poise that allowed us to stand more fully in the realisations we already carried.

> *".....what I let go of was my tendency to contract, to*

hold on, to not risk changing. The relief of finding the heart is an ecstatic release" MJ

For me, being immersed in the relational field—where the energy is one of discovery rather than declaration—allowed a softening of the habitual boundaries that would otherwise snap into place. "*Shields up,*" had been my automatic response when faced with intimacy. In this space, I found the safety to let that guard fall. It was a deep learning: that everything is actually okay.

What was also striking was how this presence began to ripple outward. People began sharing how what they were experiencing in the group was subtly transforming their relationships beyond it—affecting interactions with others who had no knowledge of what we were doing together.

> "*…I think, much as the personal boundaries between us in the group melt and dissolve in the shared experience of truth and love, I think the transparency of being is what we take out into the world and people feel it and respond to it without ever knowing what it is…*" AvV

And:

> "*…what's happening? Have people noticed changes beyond the group? I am beginning to realise some of these changes. The love we share is available to ALL. This is extraordinary but so true. I have found confidence and trust to express my experience in a way I never have before in all my life….* MJ

Graceful Navigation

What made this phase possible wasn't uniformity—people still had different temperaments, life situations, spiritual histories and unique voices that carried the depth of their own lived experiences, exploring in each moment where their understanding was leading them.

A willingness to stay responsive rather than reactive was the tone that permeated the meetings. When someone hit a challenging patch—maybe a sense of being stuck in a repeating pattern—there was room for it without the group tipping into rescue mode or analysis. Gentle reflections of how to navigate it would emerge.

When joy bubbled up, it didn't need to be explained.

When profound silence quietened everything down there was a deep respect to allow it to rest between us undisturbed.

The space between us had endless room for everything—and that made it safe.

> *"…..that was a challenging meeting…. what struck me was there was a fearlessness and honesty being expressed and I didn't feel that people were playing it safe. It felt raw and edgy but deeply real. I was quite shaken after it but, in a way, where all the pieces are thrown back up in the air and have not yet landed…." PM*

> *"…..that's what I meant about a safe space – safe to take risks because we are all pulled to those depths*

> *where we lose any identity in something deeper and more whole but forever unknown...."*

What had once felt delicate now felt surprisingly resilient. Not immune to wobble, but able to absorb it. Not rigidly harmonious, but able to return to harmony without force.

Loosening the Reins

We no longer felt the need to keep meeting behind the scenes, lightly directing the unfolding with gentle nudges

> *"When this first started, I believe all four of us were aware we were starting something that needed caring for and nurturing and to some extent guiding. But IT is growing into its own thing, and I think we can love and care for it AND take our hands off the wheel"* PM

> *"Yes, this last meeting was exponentially different – it took us further than we had all gone before (I felt)..."* AS

The Unseen Architecture

In a way, the group was becoming its own kind of organism—a shared body of awareness, each person a vital organ, each meeting a breath. We didn't talk about this explicitly, but it could be felt: a quiet coherence, woven from showing up in presence, and trusting what emerged, and a readiness to follow where it was leading.

We could almost sense the architecture of the invisible: not a system imposed from the outside, but an organic delicate structure growing from within, a living presence that for the period of the meeting gently absorbed us into its embrace and wove ever deeper connections between us—threads that kept unfolding long after the meetings ended.

Beyond the Group

Connections forged in the intimacy of the meetings had a life of their own—flowing quietly between us, unconfined by time or format.

The organic structure that had begun to emerge, was carried onward through chat apps and email exchanges, allowing the threads woven during the meetings to continue between individuals—in twos and threes—deepening relationships and carrying the field forward.

> *The conversations we've had outside of the group (and we've known each other for 30 years) are like heart surgery: I don't mean confessionals, but explorations and discoveries. We seem to clip in at a deeper level than we have ever known in the past. It isn't personal. MJ*

These unfolding conversations strengthened the sense of being part of a larger, living collective endeavour.

An Evolutionary Edge

One or two of us could feel a growing excitement. Could this space between us be a tool for evolution—not just personal, but collective?

Were we stumbling onto a deeper form of human relating that allowed the individual and the group to thrive and grow together?

We introduced the idea to the group: as before, some responded immediately, buzzing with the thrill of possibility, whilst others expressed a hesitancy and a reluctance to let go of what we were still discovering together. There was no need to force the issue. We could let it sit in the background.

The questions weren't pressing, but they hovered gently, adding a sense of sacred curiosity to our gatherings.

Reflection: Where Do You Stand?

In your own experience, can you sense the difference between simply being centred in your truth and needing to assert it? Between showing up in a group with something to prove, and simply bringing your presence as a gift?

> Try this: Think of a space where you feel free to be yourself. What qualities does it have? What makes it safe?

> Are there people in your life who carry a gentle authority—who don't dominate, but whose clarity helps others settle?

> Take a moment to stand in your own realisations. Not to push them forward, but to honour them quietly. What would it be like to move through the world from that place?

Motif 3:
The Fire Spreads –

The Courage to Expand

*"Love will arise in your heart
when you have no barrier
between yourself and another."*

— J Krishnamurti

ORIGINAL FACES

My *Original Face*
has been revealed to me.
I know the *I*
that came before the *me*.

My little life continues to unfold,
pulled this way and that by old momentums—
momentums that begin to lose their grip
beneath the steady gaze
of that which came before.

And then—
I get to sit with others
who have glimpsed their Original Face too.
Together, we cast off our masks
and bask in the quiet glory
that is revealed
when Original Faces
meet each other's eyes—
and the Vast Universe
looks back at itself.

Something Begins to open up

By this point, the group was finding a natural rhythm yet never settling into complacency.

There was always a freshness and wonder at treading new ground with every meeting, never quite knowing what territory we would explore yet trusting that the discovery would take us deeper into the field itself. We were no longer just discovering the space—we had begun to dwell in it.

> *"...I have a growing sense that the significance of the group is beyond anything we can imagine – beyond the individuals that are its building blocks. I feel simultaneously very small and also infinitely vast...." PM*

The meetings had become a focus for many of us, a kind of pulse within our lives that offered not only connection, but subtle transformation. The field was holding us and shaping us.

Taking the Risk to Grow

The question of actualising the inherent potential of our meetings, that some of us had started to sense, was hovering between us over the course of a few meetings.

> *Is this space between us more than just a backdrop? Could it be a tool for awakening in its own right?*

Could we share this space with even more people?

Maybe even people who were struggling on the path and yet to find their own inner confidence. Would the coherence and depth hold if the group expanded?

It felt risky: some of us still wanted to protect what we had, and others sensed the living invitation to open into something greater. What did become clearer over the course of a couple of discussions was that not growing might be a greater risk, the risk of stagnation—the field itself wanted to reach out further.

This question changed things. It opened a doorway.

What had been largely spontaneous began to feel intentional, even if not directed. The field wasn't just supporting our personal unfolding—it was *actively participating* in it. And more than that, it seemed to have its own impulse, its own subtle agenda.

Inviting New Members

It was this sense of a deeper intelligence moving within the group that led us to a bold decision:

> *To expand, not just by ones or twos, as previously but to take a leap and invite a group, and at the same time increase the frequency of the meetings to fortnightly to keep the growing momentum flowing.*

Over the course of two or three meetings, we invited ten new people to join. They were known to one of us through their other spiritual engagements, so there was already an alignment of sorts with what we were discovering. We invited them to share in this space as a haven from the chaos of a world in turmoil, and to find a place to encourage their own resilience and find their own voice.

They were sent a short introductory email explaining what to expect prior to their first meeting.

> *"There is no particular structure or leader, no ideology and absolutely no need to be anyone, prove anything or feel you have to jump in and be accounted for. There's lots of room just to be without any pressure or expectation.*
>
> *There is a tacit agreement to give everyone who wants to, a chance to speak by not responding too quickly or from an already familiar place and leaving lots of room for something unknown and uplifting to emerge."*

What happened surprised and delighted us. The results were astonishing.

There was no period of "settling in." From the first moments, they *felt it*—the field—and relaxed into it. Their contributions weren't tentative or performative. They spoke with clarity and vulnerability which opened the whole group up even further.

One of our new members shared her appreciation for the group in her third meeting and I asked her to offer it here:

> *"... I responded to A's call to be part of a group of recovered seekers. Right from the first virtual meeting I understood why. Instantly dropping deep into my heart, I felt immersed in a field of Love and respect and all I could share came from that place of the heart and not the intellect. The connection to this field and all the participants amazingly never goes away. It brings me a sense of belonging to the One through a circle of gentle humans sharing their findings with vulnerability and generosity. When the meeting times are coming, I rejoice like going on a date with a beloved, with the Beloved we all are, indeed. I welcome this gift with an immense gratitude. Merci la vie!" AM*

It wasn't just that they *fit in*. Their presence deepened what was already there.

Reflections and Lightbulbs

What followed were moments of shared recognition.

> *"I really enjoyed being part of the group yesterday. Not only did I experience a deep wisdom in the group field, but I also experienced a humility and kindness that the group embodied.*
>
> *Sometimes I find myself trying to push my experience in a particular direction, and sometimes even this pushing is unconscious, something I don't realize until I come into a space that's open and unjudging. In the group field, I automatically relaxed and felt that drive in me let go." JH*

Personal stories—even struggles—were brought forward, not as burdens to be solved, but as openings. Those who had faced similar challenges offered reflections—not as advice, but as deep mirroring reflecting with kindness and generosity. It wasn't about fixing or interpreting.

And you could almost see lightbulbs switch on: silent, luminous, intimate.

Deep Learning

The group meetings are dynamic spaces of real-time exploration.

There's a current of unknowingness and a vital freshness running through them—and at times, moments of quiet revelation.

There are no fixed answers. Only resonance—or sometimes even dissonance. Divergence and disagreement are not threats but invitations: to stay open, to dig deeper, to find the place that includes and transcends.

We are not uncovering rigid doctrines or rules for life. We are listening for the fluid, evolving rhythms that pulse beneath the surface of thought.

One of the quiet discoveries among us is that what makes this possible isn't special knowledge but simply being available—as we are. It's the readiness to show up, meet life—and each other—without armour, and to respond fully and fearlessly.

And then we were Sixteen

Early in April 2025, we held a meeting, our largest to date, that was a complete mix of long-term regulars and brand-new faces, some attending for the first and some for the second time.

There was quiet joy at coming together and conversation started to flow with ease as people were welcomed into the space.

What followed was a deep dive into the simplicity of resting in Being itself.

One of our regulars, a long term Zen/Dzogchen practitioner was asked to share his experience of coming through a challenging period of letting go of his many years of accumulated wisdom. His gentle tone of realising that resting as himself was not an experience, it was not supported in any way by experience, and was vast enough to accommodate everything within its boundlessness, took us deeply into a reflective space.

Someone who then spoke of bouncing 'in-and-out' of an awake state was encouraged to look deeper and as he explored his experience with us, he very clearly described recognising the moment of choice between resting in his true self and retreating to the imagined security of his mind. We reflected that he had now found the keys to the kingdom.

Over the course of about 90 minutes, fixed ideas were unravelled, blockages were shifted, and people were led back to simple moments of peace and joy mirrored back to them as gateways home.

Yes, we are Small, but….

At any one time, maybe just over half of the people on our emailing list will attend a meeting.

People lead busy lives, and this is just one element to fit into a packed schedule, often at an inconvenient time. For there is the significant challenge of meeting across multiple time zones stretching from west coast USA to east coast Australia. Inevitably there are winners and losers, and very early morning or late evening starts can be obstacles to maintaining an ongoing commitment, especially at 5am on a cold, frosty winter's morning!

And it's important to recognise that this joint endeavour isn't everyone's cup of tea.

Some who came sensed its depth but weren't quite ready to continue to engage with it. Some felt their path lay elsewhere. Others brought beautiful energy for a time, then drifted away. In all, nearly a third of the people who have passed through our portals are no longer attending, although there are still connections outside the group.

Part of the integrity of what we are discovering together, is that although it is a welcoming space for deep enquiry in which each participant is themselves part of the territory being explored, there is also a subtle austerity, that is sensitive to motivation.

There is space for our 'stories', for they are the root of personal autonomy and realness: but not as declarations of identity, instead as pathways to authenticity.

And we may be tiny, but this is a significant event nonetheless, and valuable lessons are being learned that can ripple out into the world.

Why do we Keep Coming Back?

This is not a homogenous group speaking with one single voice, constrained and controlled to mirror each other. It is a rich diversity of interested people, of all ages and backgrounds, who are willing to be transparent together, and explore, and discover something new.

I asked a few of them to share their reasons for coming back. Here are some of the different voices, all with their own perspective that produces a rich chord of coherence:

> *I tend to view each meeting as a discreet event which has its own flavour. The meetings provide a forum to meet beyond the ego/mind. For me that is the main reason for my participation. I actually feel my need for understanding has diminished over time. It may be that I have become more comfortable with not knowing. JPW*

> *"...the realization I shared in the last meeting came as a result of being in a guided meditation in the context of the spiritual healing course I'm taking. And then in this group I shared it as an idea or memory that I knew*

theoretically was somehow important, but then when speaking it developed—I believe as a result of people in the group receiving it and listening beyond the left-brain words.

So maybe that's what draws me to the group. Without such conversations I don't seem to have those kinds of reminders and discoveries. I question it though because nothing seems to "stick" and I return to being my usual psychologically compromised, unenlightened self when alone and back in my own solitary head!..... I need to engage more with others to bring it forward, albeit temporarily." WB

At our meeting this past weekend, I was struck again by the openness in the field of the group. I felt a holding of support, as well as an underlying love for people as they were. A lovely feeling, actually…… The field itself is lovely.

No one is judging or preaching, and no one is trying to impress. There's simply the sharing of wisdom and gentle encouragement…… The lack of grandstanding and the presence of humility is very strong in this group, and it's something that I particularly resonate with.

I look forward to the meetings and find myself drawn to the wisdom embodied in the field itself. There are the words that are said, and then there's the feeling of the field itself, and if I'm being honest, it's the feeling of the field itself that has an effect on my own understanding.

Something in me recognizes the wisdom in the field and relaxes the part of me that gets caught up in the Trying and the Doing, and then the underlying wisdom itself comes forward and relaxes everything in me. It's the relaxing that usually brings forward understanding for me.

I think it's good for people to meet and to talk about what can be a very solitary experience. Things happen to us on this journey that don't make sense to other people and oftentimes don't make sense to ourselves. To have a space to talk and discuss these things is very precious, and to have them led by people who have a deep understanding, and a warm open heartedness is very rare. JH

A Living Invitation

We're still in the midst of this expansion, and we're learning as we go.

There are no final conclusions to draw. It feels like a work in progress—and perhaps it always will.

But what is clear is that the field has resilience. It can stretch and include more without losing its essence. Indeed, as it grows, its presence seems to deepen and widen and vibrate with inherent potential.

And as the field strengthens, so too do we—becoming more sensitive, more transparent, more confident in our openness. The resilience of the field seems to awaken a matching trust within us: to show up more fully, to reveal more honestly, and to listen with the whole of our being.

Those with more experience now help to guide the flow and hold the focus—never by taking over, but by creating spaces of safety and subtle encouragement. These open moments invite others, especially those less confident, to begin expressing in their own words what is being revealed to them. In this gentle atmosphere of exploration, something deeper stirs: a chance to speak from authenticity, to meet their own realness with curiosity, and to begin recognising the self that has been quietly waiting beneath the noise.

Moments of deep resonance almost stun the group, when a particular phrase or way of expressing something rings with such freshness, authenticity, and clarity—like the gasp of amazement from hitting the bullseye square in the centre. Sometimes, it's more like the deep vibration of a temple bell, echoing through the precincts and bringing everything to a quiet pause, as if inviting a breath of collective contemplation.

It may be that the next stage of our evolution isn't individual at all. It may happen *between us*—in the space where no one is trying to lead or follow, but where all are rooted in the awareness that came before the 'me'.

Holding the Flame

As one of the original four, I always feel a deep responsibility for the space—not out of obligation, but from love. I'm aware of it to some degree all the time in the background of my experience, even outside the meetings. It doesn't belong to us. We are simply its stewards.

A Message Wanting to Be Shared

This may be why I feel so drawn to write about it. The desire to share this with others, to invite more people into this discovery, feels like it's coming from the field itself. It's not just for us. It wants to be lived and known more widely.

Reflection: A Field That Evolves

Take a few moments and consider:

> What if the most transformative experiences don't come from a teacher, a book, or even a meditation cushion—but from how we meet one another?

> Have you ever felt something sacred or intelligent in the quality of a shared space?

> What would it take to trust that this field knows more than you do?

If the answer comes in silence, let it. The field is listening.

Transition into the Second Movement: Digging Deeper

As we turn now from the lived rhythm of this group's unfolding to consider the deeper patterns beneath it, we begin to ask:

> *Why now? Why this*
> *What is it about our moment in history—*
> *and our moment in consciousness—*
> *that encourages such a shared field to appear?*

This next movement explores some of the underlying dynamics:

—the quiet mystery that can arise between us,
—the importance of walking our own path with integrity
—the cultural and personal patterns that shape—and often limit—how we relate.

In many ways, it's the broader landscape in which this fire has found room to grow.

Second Movement – Digging Deeper –

Finding the Context

*"The greatest revolution of our time is
the discovery that human beings,
by changing the inner attitudes of their minds,
can change the outer aspects of their lives."*

— William James

GRANT UNTO OTHERS

Grant unto others
the silent mystery
that is the screen of my experience—
the vast open space
no longer preoccupied with what I want,
but open to all possibilities.

Others may not recognise it in themselves,
but it is there, nonetheless—
who they truly are
beneath the smokescreen
of clung-to identity.

The deeper I dive into my experience,
the simpler the understanding becomes:
Emptiness meeting Wholeness
in an intimate embrace.
Wisdom and Compassion,
forever entwined like the caduceus.

How is Emptiness known?
As the fluidity of no inner resistance.
And how does Wholeness appear
to eyes that only see
the multitudes of creation?
As the Ground of Being
shining through all—
whether they know it or not.

'No resistance' is beyond will,
beyond choice,
beyond even the saying of "Yes" or "No"
to experience itself.
It is the Ground of Being.
And Diversity—
is the radiant expression
of the Infinite Heart.

Motif 4:
The Mystery Between Us –

Awakening as Relationship

*"The meeting of two personalities is like
the contact of two chemical substances:
if there is any reaction, both are transformed."*

— C.G. Jung

HOLD THIS SPACE

In the acceptance of *What Is*,
in the natural surrender that follows
the recognition of one's Original Face,
the world appears changed.

It comes alive.
There is a tingle in the air,
an electric current of vitality infuses the view,
and a deep sense of sacred, precious immediacy
makes everything sing a hymn of praise
to Divine Presence.

Hold this space.
Anyone who steps into its orbit will sense it
somewhere in their being—
even if not yet consciously.

Hold this space.
Share it with awakened souls who glimpse the same view.
Create a networked alternative reality:
a living unity,
a between-space of perfect stillness,
transforming the world
through a shared seeing
with many connected eyes.

Hold this space.
Let us change the world—
from the inside out.

Introduction: Awakening in Relationship

For centuries, humanity has struggled to find harmony between the rights and freedoms of the individual and the deep need for belonging in a community.

We have witnessed this conflict in politics, culture, and philosophy. Today, this tension has reached a fever pitch, as polarization deepens fragmentation, and social media isolates us in silos, fomenting conflict rather than resolution.

But in the midst of this crisis, there is an invitation to explore and share in a new way of being together—one that transcends these divides, inviting us to meet in the mysterious, luminous space between us, where connection and awakening are possible.

The Space Between Us: More Than Just Physical Proximity

This space between us is not just empty air; it is a living field of infinite potential, waiting to be revealed when we let go of the need to already know.

When we engage with each other beyond our fixed identities, we open to a new way of relating—one that holds both personal autonomy and shared belonging.

Throughout history, we have seen the pendulum swing between these two forces, but now, at this moment, there is an emerging opportunity to step beyond this duality and into a space of mutual awakening.

The Role of Presence: The Art of Truly Being with Others

True presence is the art of meeting another without the need for performance or validation.

It is to show up, fully aware of one's own vulnerabilities, without trying to control the situation. This vulnerability not only deepens connection but also creates a living space of trust where both the individual and the collective can thrive and evolve.

In this space, we surrender the need to be right, opening the way for something greater than ourselves to emerge.

Surrendering to "The Space Between Us"

Our egos resist this kind of connection because of the fear of losing control, of losing the sense of individuality.

Yet, it is in surrendering this illusion of control that we enter the deepest form of connection, a true communion. The space between us becomes a place where we are no longer defined by our individual narratives, but by something deeper—our shared humanity.

In letting go of ego's need to define, protect, or perform, we open the door to a new kind of relational freedom, one that honours both our uniqueness and our belonging.

The Alchemy of Connection: What Happens in the Space Between?

Meeting each other in the space between, we are engaged in an alchemical process.

Our connection becomes the catalyst for transformation—both for us as individuals, and for the relationship, and ultimately, for the collective we belong to.

In this sacred space, we no longer come together for transactional reasons, but for the deeper purpose of mutual awakening. It is here, in the relational field, that we discover a new way of being together—one that transcends the divisions of our time and points toward a more harmonious future.

Practicing the Mystery: How to Hold the Space with Others

To begin practicing the mystery of connection, start by simply being present.

> In your conversations, practice deep listening.
>
> Pay attention not only to what is being said, but also to the energy beneath the words.
>
> Let go of any desire to be seen, to fix, or to subtly guide the other person.
>
> Create space for the other to simply be and allow yourself to be held in that same space.

With time, this practice dissolves the invisible walls that keep us apart, and the space between becomes a field of awakening.

The Invitation to Explore the Mystery

This chapter has only scratched the surface of what is possible when we enter the space between. I hope you feel the pull to follow this further.

The invitation is here:

> Might you meet others in this sacred space of presence and vulnerability?
>
> Will you allow yourself to be transformed by the alchemy of true connection?

The journey begins here—together, in the mystery between us.

Reflection: Listening Without an Agenda

Take a moment today to engage with someone in a way that maybe you haven't before.

Approach the conversation not as a means to get something from the other person, but simply to be fully present.

Listen deeply, without interrupting or anticipating.

Let go of what you feel you must say.

Notice what shifts in the space between you and reflect on how this practice might shift the dynamics of your relationships.

Stepping Through

In stepping into this space of possibility—where something new wants to emerge between us—we begin to sense that awakening is not only a private journey, but a shared unfolding.

And yet, the path to that shared space is not found by abandoning ourselves.

Rather, it begins right where we are, in the very heart of our lived experience. As we turn inward with curiosity and courage, we may discover that our most personal truths carry within them the very signature of the universal.

In the next chapter, we'll explore how walking our unique path becomes the gateway to something far greater than ourselves.

Motif 5:
Your Path is the Portal –

Authenticity is the Key to the Kingdom

"Be yourself. Everyone else is already taken."

— Oscar Wilde

THE UNIQUE IS THE UNIVERSAL

Once the heart-longing for liberation is ignited,
each of us walks a unique path—unfolding one step at a time.

The destination is the Universal Heart
beating at the core of our Being.

Our starting points are many,
our journeys wind across different terrains,
each filled with distinct challenges.

We each have our own demons to face,
and our own strengths and talents to discover.

Beware: *unique* does not mean *special*.
The need to feel special is the root of all conflict.

Trust your own experience.
Find your inner guide.
That's the key to discovering commonality with others.

Authenticity is your direct expression of the Universal—
not through comparison or imitation,
but through the living truth of your own being.

Sing your own song, straight from the heart,
and the harmony that arises as others sing theirs is divine.

The rhythm of your heart is what connects you to others—
and a Sangha of brothers and sisters is born.

Relax.
Your unique expression is the very thing
that allows you to find your place
in the great unfolding of the Universal.

Introduction: Unrepeatable You

Each of us carries an unrepeatable perspective, shaped by the terrain of our lives.

Often, we are taught to see this uniqueness as a barrier to unity—as if being different means being separate.

But what if our individuality is not a deviation from the universal, but a *portal into it?* What if, in fully embodying our own path, we simultaneously become available to something much greater than ourselves?

This chapter explores how authenticity is not isolation, but the very *means* by which we participate in shared presence. It is in walking our own path with integrity that we become receptive to the deeper field of human interconnection.

The Myth of Separation Through Comparison

From childhood, we're subtly trained to compare ourselves to others:

> To measure, to strive, to "fit in."
> Uniqueness becomes a source of anxiety rather than celebration.
> We learn to hide our differences or to amplify them in ways that seek validation.
> But both hiding and performing keep us distanced from genuine connection.

When we abandon comparison and drop into the texture of our own life, something remarkable happens: we begin to feel *real*.

And in that reality, we can sense the universal. The very thing we thought separated us—our individuality—turns out to be the very path into resonance with others.

Authenticity as an Invitation to the Field

When we meet someone who is deeply themselves—not performing, not fixing, not seeking approval—we recognise it and sense an invitation to do the same.

Something softens. The social mask begins to fall away. We feel a kind of welcome into presence, not just with that person but with something larger—a *field of awareness* that doesn't belong to either of us but arises *between* us.

This is where interbeing begins: not by discarding ourselves, but by becoming so rooted in our authenticity that we no longer need to protect it.

Trusting the Living Thread of Your Path

Your life, in all its specificity, has prepared you for this moment.

The joys, the failures, the unexpected turns—each one has contributed to a thread of being that only you carry.

When you trust this thread, and stop trying to replicate someone else's journey, you arrive at a place where your path begins to *resonate with others*, not because it's the same, but because it's real.

As Paula D'Arcy so poignantly expressed, "*God comes to you disguised as your life*". Your own experience, just as it is, becomes your doorway.

Together, we are weaving a tapestry of such infinite complexity, and those moments of resonance between us create zones of harmony, clarity and beauty within the chaos that so often confuses and overwhelms.

The universal doesn't flatten us into sameness—it welcomes our differences into a larger pattern.

Like notes in a chord, our uniqueness becomes part of the music of the whole.

No Pretence

Our individual authenticity, our own unique journeys, our specific talents and interests and life experiences and the honesty to stand in them and as them, is the only place we can meet others without pretence, without games, without the need to hide. It is as if each of us uncovers our true light and together the glow is magnificent.

> *...being in a group like this is remembering our true nature through exchanging, listening, questioning and...being together in silence.*

It is recognising that there is nowhere to go, nothing to strive for, nothing much to do. That we are home, just as we are, with our differences, preferences, ways of expressing. That spiritual life really is embracing day to day life - the only life we have- with experiences as they come, regardless.

Instead of hunting for blissful explosions or reaching out for some special state, that — who knows — just as well might be another ego trick.

Sharing that realisation, by being together, is relaxing in liberation.

Allowing each other to be whoever, sharing the profound yet simple wisdom that our individual lives are manifestations from the source, that cannot be described with words.

That we are deeply connected and that we all add our specific colour and value. The support, the friendship, the respect and humility. I love it. The beauty of this group is that it surpasses doubt or cynicism in a split second, because of the recognition and mutually experienced memory.

And because we read in each other's eyes that we know, that we can trust and that there's a whole lot of helping hands.

Even though we are continents apart, connected through a communication app, there's always immediacy and profound connection in the now. AvV

We meet in our realness—in the texture of our messy humanity—and there we find a living truth. Not a manufactured perfection, but a felt sense of wholeness. A quiet goodness that includes everything just as it is.

Radical Personal Autonomy: The Courage to Be Authentic

This journey toward authenticity requires what might be called "radical personal autonomy"—the courage to stand in one's own experience even when the collective current flows elsewhere.

It is not the rugged individualism celebrated in Western culture, but rather the willingness to trust one's own being, even when doing so feels risky.

In group settings, there is often subtle pressure to conform, to align with the prevailing narrative. The paradox is that true connection becomes possible precisely when we resist this pressure—when we honour our unique perspective while remaining open to others.

This autonomy isn't about separation; it's about integrity. And integrity is what makes us available for the deeper forms of connection. As we learn to trust our inner compass, we discover that the more firmly we stand in our own truth, the more genuinely we can meet others in theirs.

Reflection: Rooting into Your Realness

Take a moment today to reflect on a time when you felt most *yourself*—not the self shaped by expectations or performance, but the self that simply *is*. What were you doing? How did it feel in your body? Who were you with?

Now consider how you might bring more of that realness into your interactions. In your next conversation, try letting go of the need to impress or explain. Let your words arise from presence. Notice what shifts—not just in you, but in the space between you.

Relax into your Uniqueness

But if our uniqueness is the very gateway to connection, why do we so often hide it, mistrust it, or feel unsafe expressing it?

The paradox lies in our relationship with our own authenticity. What should bring us closer—our genuine self-expression—often becomes what creates distance.

This distance emerges from a fundamental misunderstanding: that our uniqueness separates us from others, rather than connects us to the universal. We learn to see our differences as barriers rather than as essential threads in the weaving of the tapestry of human experience.

In this misunderstanding, we begin to craft personas rather than express our essence. We develop strategies of connection that prevent the very intimacy we seek. The authentic self becomes hidden beneath layers of adaptation and performance.

These adaptations aren't arbitrary—they're responses to environments where our full expression felt unwelcome or unsafe. They served a purpose in their time. But what once protected us now confines us.

To understand this confinement, we must look deeper—into the cultural, psychological, and spiritual patterns that have taught us to fear our own essence and guard against others.

These patterns are not personal failings; they are inherited wounds, collective traumas, and ancient survival strategies. They have shaped our sense of self in ways that cut us off from the ground of being.

In the next chapter, we explore the deeper patterns of separation that have shaped our sense of self and our ways of relating—and how presence offers a pathway back to wholeness.

Motif 6:
The Roots of Separation –

Dropping the Masks of Otherness

"We are not human beings having a spiritual experience. We are spiritual beings having a human experience."

— Pierre Teilhard de Chardin

AUTHENTICITY

Intimacy—true intimacy—arises in vulnerability and transparency,
when individuals who have discovered
their authentic, undefinable self
meet one another beyond performance.
Something new becomes possible:
a radical way to inter-relate, to dialogue,
to discover creative, embodied responses
to the challenges of this world.

This intimacy demands radical personal autonomy—
a balance between deep humility
(seeing 'that which is beyond' as the true author),
and the courage to shine—
to stand in what has been discovered as true.
It's a kind of living that invites risk—
and may provoke reactions of both praise and disapproval.

It asks for inner integrity,
a vastness of reflection,
and a willingness to question everything,
again and again and again.
It is a quiet rebellion
against the conditioning to conform—
a refusal to surrender one's conscience
to a louder voice.
It asks for vigilance, for presence,
for clarity in the face of the crowd.

"Know Thyself"
has never been more vital.

We stand at a crossroads.
Groupthink dominates the political landscape.
Culture wars feed on difference
and forget our shared human ground.
Individuality has been swallowed—
subsumed by charismatic leaders
into homogeneous, aggressive movements.

Belonging to the tribe
has, for now, triumphed
over the liberal instinct
toward individual freedom.
Idealised abstractions are enforced as virtue—
disconnected from the messy beauty
of what it means to be truly human.

History has always swung
between self and group,
between autonomy and conformity.
But perhaps this is the moment
not for more swinging,
but for integration.

Do we have the heart
—and the courage—
to meet each other
beyond our fiercely held identities?

Can we drop our defences,
relinquish our prejudices,
and see through the veils
of conditioning and unconscious bias?

In that deep vulnerability,
might we discover an unimagined reality—
one, where personal freedom
is not in opposition to belonging,
but its very foundation?

It has the power to change the world.

The Pain of Disconnection

Before we can fully enter the shared field of awakening, we must acknowledge the deep fragmentation many of us carry—personally and collectively.

These fractures show up in our thoughts, emotions, relationships, and culture. They shape our sense of self and disconnect us from the world around us.

Often, this disconnection is felt first as a vague unease, or as a sense of not quite belonging—of having to wear a mask just to get by. It can start early, in the playground, as we learn to conform, compete, or hide.

This chapter explores how our personal wounds echo larger cultural patterns, and how our longing for wholeness is not naïve, but deeply intelligent.

Wounds That Whisper: The Personal Roots

Most of us carry subtle (and not-so-subtle) emotional imprints from our earliest years.

> *Perhaps it was a moment of rejection, of being misunderstood, or of learning that our authenticity made others uncomfortable.*

These moments often taught us to fragment ourselves—to suppress what was real in order to feel safe or accepted. These are not just individual experiences—they are deeply human ones. In trying to be loved or included, we may have traded in our spontaneity for approval.

The cost? A growing distance from our true nature.

But the whisper of the real self never fully disappears. It surfaces in moments of stillness, longing, or when life cracks us open.

Culture as Amplifier: The Pressure to Perform

Our culture rewards appearance over essence. It favours performance over presence, branding over being.

In such a landscape, we learn to craft identities rather than inhabit selves. We curate, polish, and protect an image, (or even multiple images for different circumstances), that we hope will shield us from rejection.

This pressure to perform doesn't just amplify our inner wounds—it normalizes them. We mistake fitting in for belonging, and success for self-worth. But deep down, something in us resists. We long for something real.

The Challenges of The Digital Age

The digital age has intensified our separation patterns to an unprecedented degree. Social media platforms encourage carefully curated versions of ourselves, optimized for likes rather than authentic expression. We become personal brands constantly monitoring our "performance metrics" through followers and digital validation.

This performance extends into our work lives, where

we're increasingly visible and measurable. Video calls bring colleagues into our homes, while productivity software tracks our output. We've become accountable to a spreadsheet mentality—one that has edited out the compassion and empathy at the heart of our humanity. The boundary between authentic self and professional persona blurs.

Even our intimate relationships aren't immune. Dating apps turn connection into a marketplace, where the superficial replaces the real and disinhibition thrives behind screens. In the absence of face-to-face nuance, impulses once softened by social convention now surface unchecked. Texting creates permanent records of conversations that once would have been ephemeral. Spontaneity—the lifeblood of authentic connection—is increasingly squeezed out. We are adrift, disconnected from anything that might feel truly real. No wonder mental health challenges, especially among the young, are reaching epidemic levels.

These patterns reshape our collective landscape. Political discourse becomes performative, with substance sacrificed for shareable soundbites. Complex issues reduce to binary positions. The fabric of shared reality frays as we retreat into information bubbles.

Digital Paradox: Connection Through Technology

Yet paradoxically, these same digital tools can become

vessels for authentic connection. Our own group demonstrates this possibility—meeting through Zoom, staying connected via WhatsApp and email, yet still accessing profound levels of presence and intimacy.

The difference lies not in the technology itself, but in how we use it. When we approach digital spaces with the same intention, presence, and authenticity that we bring to in-person gatherings, something remarkable happens. The medium fades into the background, and real connection emerges.

In this fractured context, the journey toward authentic connection becomes both more challenging and more vital. The skills we develop in our group—deep listening, presence, the courage to be real—aren't just personal growth tools. They're essential capacities for healing our wider culture.

When we drop the performance and meet in authenticity, we practice a new way of being human together—one that might begin to heal the deeper patterns of separation threatening our collective wellbeing.

This isn't about rejecting technology. It's about bringing awareness to how we engage with it. It's about creating spaces—both physical and virtual—where different values flourish: presence over performance, depth over display, authenticity over approval.

In these spaces, we remember what it means to be human together. And that remembering ripples outward, touching everything we do.

The Machinery of Identity

At the heart of this fragmentation is a subtle but powerful illusion:

> *That the self is a fixed entity. Thought loops reinforce this idea, creating an internal commentator that narrates, judges, and strategizes. Over time, we begin to believe that this voice is who we are.*

But awareness doesn't arise *from* this voice—it holds it. The voice is *not* the self. When we see this clearly, a shift begins. It can feel disorienting, even terrifying, to loosen our grip on our familiar identity structures we've built. But it's also the beginning of freedom.

The Crisis and the Invitation

Recognizing the illusion doesn't mean it instantly disappears. For most of us, there's a back-and-forth—insight followed by regression, clarity followed by confusion. This is not failure. It's the rhythm of awakening. And it is a learning curve, consolidating a deeper pattern, that strengthens with every set-back and return to the fray.

What's needed here is not perfection, but *trust*. The courage to keep showing up. The humility to keep watching. The honesty to admit when we've slipped back into the mask—and the compassion to return, again and again, to presence.

The First Signs of Wholeness

Something new begins to stir as we see through the old patterns.

Spaciousness opens up. Reactions lose their grip. There are moments—sometimes fleeting—when we feel at home in ourselves, without even knowing exactly who that self is.

These moments matter. They are the early signs of re-integration. Not because we've figured it all out, but because we've stopped resisting what is.

The Cost of Forgetting

Our fragmentation—both personal and collective—is not a flaw in our design. It is the residue of adaptation, the cost of forgetting who and what we really are in order to survive.

But remembering is possible.

We are not static selves trapped in a narrative. We are dynamic beings, unfolding in relationship—with each other, with life, and with the deeper ground of awareness that holds it all.

To glimpse this ground is to begin to heal. To explore it with others passionately engaged in the same unravelling is to share the burden, and to rest in it together is to come home.

Dissolving the Illusion of Separation

When we gather in the field of shared presence, something remarkable begins to happen to the ways we hold ourselves separate. Like ice meeting warmth, what was rigid and fixed starts to soften and flow.

This transformation isn't intellectual—it's experiential. It happens not through analysis or process or strategy, but through direct encounter—with ourselves and with each other—in a space of non-judgment and deep listening.

The process appears to unfold in layers:

First comes recognition. In the clarity of being together, we begin to notice our habits of separation—the subtle ways we withdraw, defend, perform, or compare. These patterns, once invisible because they were so constant, suddenly stand in relief against the backdrop of presence.

 It can be frightening to confront this initially, for the habit is ingrained, but the invitation of this subtle relational space is gentle and affirming and confidence building.

Next comes a gentle holding. The field itself seems to create an ambiance strong enough to hold these patterns without judgment. Unlike our usual self-improvement projects, which often carry subtle self-rejection and forceful imposition, this is a spacious allowing—a compassionate witnessing that doesn't demand immediate change.

Within this kind of presence, something begins to unwind, knots of anxious response unravel, an unconscious tension relaxes. The energy once locked in keeping us defended—vigilance, performance, constant self-monitoring—starts to release. There's a palpable sense of relief, of coming home to ourselves.

As these patterns begin to dissolve, new possibilities emerge. Connections that once seemed impossible become natural. Conversations that would have triggered defensiveness unfold with surprising ease. The very differences that once threatened now enrich.

This is not a linear process with a clear endpoint. It's more like a spiral, returning to similar territory but at deeper levels. Old patterns may resurface, especially under stress, but they no longer hold the same power. We notice them more quickly, meet them more softly, and return to relational awareness with greater ease.

What makes this transformation so dynamic is that it's not happening in isolation. The very act of being witnessed, of unfolding together in real time, changes the terrain. There's a profound difference between struggling with our separation mechanisms in isolation and unwinding them together in the light of mutual awareness. Indeed, being together is the perfect mirror to shine a light on these unconscious reflexes that aren't immediately apparent to us when alone.

In the field, our individual healing becomes collective healing. As one person finds the courage to drop a mask, others recognize the same pattern in themselves. As one person speaks from authentic vulnerability, the entire field deepens in its capacity to hold complexity and truth.

This is how presence transforms separation—not by forcing change or demanding perfection, but by creating conditions where our natural wholeness can re-emerge. Not by adding something new, by dissolving what obscures the wholeness that's already here.

The journey from fragmentation to wholeness isn't about becoming someone different. It's about returning to who we already are beneath the layers of protection and performance. It's about remembering our essential nature— and seeing it mirrored in each other.

Reflection: Meeting the Mask

Think of a situation where you often feel the need to perform or hide. What are you afraid might happen if you showed up without the mask? What part of you is trying to protect you? What part feels the need for protection? And from what?

Now bring kind attention to that part. Let it know you see it, understand its efforts, and are willing to meet the moment with a little more truth. Even a small step toward authenticity can begin to change the shape of your inner world.

Maybe you could invite a close friend to explore this with you and investigate together what keeps you separate and what brings you more closely together

Transition into the Third Movement: The Far Horizon

As we move through the mystery of shared presence, we begin to sense that this field is not a fleeting glimpse, but the early flowering of a new way of being.

Like tender shoots nurtured in a greenhouse, these discoveries are still vulnerable—yet they carry the potential to take root and thrive in the wider world.

In the next section, we explore how to bring this way of relating into the open air of daily life.

> What does it take to sustain the field when challenges arise?
> How do we prune what no longer serves, and nourish what is alive and true?

The practice of shared awakening is not a fixed path but a living garden—responsive, seasonal, and always growing.

Third Movement – The Far Horizon –

Seeding the New

"When a complex system is far from equilibrium, small islands of coherence in a sea of chaos, have the capacity to shift the entire system, to a higher order."

— Ilya Prigogine, Nobel Prize-winning chemist

AWAKENED LIVING

There is a discovery with the power
to catalyse radical change,
rippling outward like waves
from a stone cast into water.

It is not a discovery one makes alone,
but an arising that happens between—
a current flowing through those who gather
within a shared, alchemical space.

It is a field of awakening,
and once ignited, once embodied
by a core group devoted to its emergence,
it resonates, deep and clear—
like a tuning fork, setting strings to vibrate,
transmitting the clarity, peace, and open sensibility
that mark an awakened presence.

It holds a wisdom beyond any single mind,
expressed with a warm humility
that does not judge but deepens understanding.
In this inviting embrace,
newcomers feel the pull to leave their baggage at the shore
and dive into the bottomless ocean of Being—together.

It is not the surrender of personal autonomy.
Quite the opposite.
Each must take the risk to stand in their own realization,
to explore what unfolds from a place of not-already-knowing.
Shedding the suffocating layers of self-concern,

one uncovers the authenticity already present—
and in doing so, sees more clearly:
there is only one authentic self,
expressing through a thousand voices.
It is the harmony of a synchronous choir,
singing a multi-layered oratorio.

It requires only a few conditions to arise:
a willingness to truly listen,
to pick up a thread and follow where it leads,
or dive deeper into what has been spoken.
A willingness to be vulnerable, honest and bare,
to stand in truth without armour.
A willingness to abandon cherished ideas,
to look and listen with fresh eyes and ears.

And then—no matter your past, your tribe, your faith—
you stand naked and alone,
yet deeply at one with others, equally transparent.

It is a wonder.
And as it spreads, widening its embrace,
the world itself awakens.

Motif 7:
The Emergent Field –

Coherence, a Living Mystery

"We need evolutionary coherence: not the monoculture of agreement, but a harmonization of complex, multi-perspectival truths."

— Terry Patten – *A New Republic of the Heart*

DEEPER AWAKENING

We meet and explore our direct experience of the unknown
and together discover a transcendent dimension—
of peace, silence, simple joy and a depth beyond measure—
that words can barely touch.
Words only hint at the living electricity that flows between us.

We are all impacted.
We know something significant has occurred—
and is reproducible,
as we continue to rediscover, again and again,
the many facets of its extraordinary ordinariness.

But is there more?

Each of us turns up, participates, and then leaves—
each must drop some boundaries—if only for a while—
risk vulnerability to taste the inter-personal
and touch the deeper shared layer of self.

We navigate our own fears and intuitions,
reach beyond the prison of the personal.
Yet traces remain—
the uniqueness of our standpoints not quite surrendered,
even in the recognition of something more.

Does our shared experience point to a deeper awakening?
If asked, we would all say we know:
there is only one "I"
with many windows onto the eternal present.

But there may be a deeper realisation:
that the group itself is the common "I"—
not something we're part of,
but something we are,
each of us the whole of it.

A deeper layer of the formless
taking form as a union of individuals.
Perhaps both an explosion and a profound emptiness.
Perhaps a responsibility that lingers between meetings.
Whatever it is—
I'm truly excited
and magnetically pulled
to find out.

A Quiet Shift

Something has subtly changed.

The early flickers of intimacy, described in previous chapters, have become something more sustained, more luminous.

As the group has matured, so too has the quality of our meetings. We find ourselves navigating the relational field with growing ease, like swimmers who have become familiar with the currents.

The silences hum with presence. Contributions land more deeply. The sense of a shared intelligence that embraces us all has become quietly, unmistakably alive.

From Unfolding to Participation

Could it be that this space is no longer simply emerging, but beginning to reveal its own integrity—a coherence that is not imposed but discovered?

> *"The group seems to self-regulate to a certain degree, not through rules or roles, but through trust. What once required courage now feels like a natural way of being."*
> PM

And within this unfolding, we're discovering something even more surprising: the field seems to want to grow, not necessarily in size but in depth. Not out of ambition, but out of a quiet, pressing invitation.

And as it grows, so do those of us engaging with it. The same coherence that supports the group also supports each person within it—opening new capacities for presence, deepening self-trust, and inviting a more grounded, transparent way of being. Growth here doesn't feel driven; it feels discovered, like something already waiting inside us.

It may be fanciful… or perhaps we are witnessing the birth of a new kind of 'We'.

A Loosening of Personal Identity

One of the gentlest shifts—almost imperceptible—is in how we each relate to ourselves.

There's a softening. A relaxation of the need to hold firm to our own story, our own insight, our own role—the need to be a someone.

Some of us have spoken about feeling part of a larger Self. Not losing our individuality, but including it in a wider, more fluid sense of identity.

Within the group, this loosening of personal boundaries becomes part of the learning. Not a concept, but a lived experience—where identity expands, softens, and sometimes dissolves in the presence of deep trust.

In a recent meeting, in the quiet of spontaneous meditation at the end of the session, I saw my face in a little box on the screen and didn't recognise it as 'me'—there was only the undefinable sense of being rooted in the awareness that was witnessing it all: the screen, the faces, the meeting, and the world in which it was all arising.

Is this what awakening together might look like?

Listening to the Field

We're not following a plan.

The field itself seems to offer subtle signals—nudges felt sometimes individually, and sometimes collectively.

As one of the original members, I've found myself sensing this space even between meetings, as if it were an invisible presence humming just beneath daily life.

The meetings run on their own rhythm now, not awaiting a call or a leader, but arising from something deeper. When someone new joins and immediately relaxes into presence, when a wordless silence fills the screen, when spontaneous clarity arises across the group—what are we witnessing?

Could it be that the field has become a kind of lineage—not passed down from person to person, but carried as a continuous flow of presence, directly from that first spark between four friends?

It feels so different from the old paradigm of transmission. Just something new arising… when we meet each other without defence.

Becoming Resonant Instruments

This is not to say that the field teaches us directly—but it certainly gives us the courage, confidence and readiness to share our lived experience more openly, with a sense of active enquiry not as a pre-packaged module. It optimises the inherent potential in each of us to discover our deeper collective intelligence and, it feels bold to say it out loud, but to speak from the one heart.

Something in the space welcomes vulnerability, invites inquiry, and from this quality of listening and responding, wisdom emerges—not from one person, but from the resonance between us.

It's less about transmitting knowledge and more about co-creating understanding and allowing it to take us deeper.

This isn't the old spiritual model of guru to student, but a more democratic, relational transmission.

There is no one who holds the power, although those with more experience in the space and possibly more finely tuned to its potential can gently guide and direct as needed.

The power arises when we meet in authenticity and coherence and trust in our own inner voice as it resonates with the emergence between us.

> *Could it be that this field is part of something larger—an evolutionary movement toward greater coherence, communion, and relational intelligence?*

We don't know. But we keep showing up, drawn by a quiet sense that we're part of something meaningful.

Tending the Flame

We don't know where this is going, and that feels like a strength.

At each stage in the group's unfolding there has been a subtle intuition of what might be next, a sense at the edge of awareness, of something calling us forward. Not necessarily sensed by all but introduced to the group with care and generosity by those who have felt that call.

The desire to hold on to certainty has given way to a participatory curiosity. It's a dynamic interplay building on the confidence gained but led forward by the thrill of discovering the new. Perhaps what we're practicing isn't just presence, but a trust in what emerges when we're fully here, together.

Maybe an evolution in relationship can deepen what it means to be human together.

It feels as if the universe is leaning in.

Reflection:

What would it mean for you to listen not just to the people around you, but to the subtle space between?

Can you notice the quiet impulses that arise when you're fully present with others—those nudges that feel less like your own and more like a shared knowing?

Have you ever found yourself saying something in a group you didn't expect to say—and it felt like exactly what was needed?

Try entering a conversation today without an agenda. Follow the thread of what wants to emerge.

Motif 8:
A New Way of Awakening –

Resonance as Transmission

"To listen is to lean in, softly, with a willingness to be changed by what we hear."

— Mark Nepo

INSTANT INTIMACY

Intimacy has nothing to do
with history, memory, identity, or time.

It is the instantaneous dissolving of boundaries
that protect the false sense of self.
It is the immediate recognition, in the other,
that there is no other.

It is sharing in the infinite potentials of being human—
through not knowing who you are
(in any definable sense),
yet fully knowing who you are
(in the resting as pure Being).

It is sensing the One Heart beating together,
enjoying the natural joy, peace, stillness, and silence
that connect us at the deepest level.

It is meeting beyond concept.
It cannot be generated.
There is no strategy.
Time does not feature.

It is the universal, flowing through limitless space
when the prison walls of the mind dissolve.

A World on Fire

At the time of writing, our world stands at a precipice. Across the globe, we witness the rise of tribalism, the hardening of borders both physical and ideological, and the growing appeal of authoritarian certainty over democratic complexity. Many are drawn to apocalyptic narratives—stories that justify destruction in service of a promised renewal that always seems to require someone else's sacrifice.

The post-war international order is unravelling. Institutions designed to uphold human rights and prevent conflict are weakening under the weight of competing interests and eroding trust. Nations that once championed universal principles increasingly apply them selectively, creating a crisis of moral leadership that reverberates through our collective consciousness.

Personal autonomy struggles against powerful currents pulling us toward group identities and tribal allegiances. The spaces for nuanced thought contract as public discourse becomes increasingly binary and combative. Meanwhile, beneath the surface of our social media feeds, isolation deepens, mental health crises multiply, and the fundamental human need for genuine connection goes unmet.

This is Thanatos: the death-drive that exists within all human systems—the impulse that would rather destroy than transform, that clings to familiar patterns even as they lead toward collapse.

And yet—against this backdrop—something else is quietly emerging, almost under the radar.

Eros: the life force itself. The impulse toward renewal, integration, and the birth of something wholly new.

Eros does not fight Thanatos head-on. It does not argue. It simply lives more fully—spacious, creative, irrepressibly alive. It doesn't oppose; it responds. It brings something new into being and carries light into darkness.

Sparks Through the Cracks

Could it be that what we're experiencing in our group is not a retreat from the world, but a response to it? Not a reaction to the challenges but a creative flowering opening new possibilities.

Small constellations of people gathering across borders, meeting via the digital interconnectivity which is so much a feature of our times.

> No ideology. No leader. No dogma.
> Just presence.
> And a growing recognition that meeting each other in authenticity and silence—without strategy or defensiveness—might be the very thing that helps us remember who we are.

Is an invisible current of coherence threading itself through the chaos of these times?

As the long-established structures of social order collapse like dominoes, there are cracks appearing, through which something new can emerge.

Might this intersubjective coherence offer a different kind of response—one rooted not in opposition, but in presence? Can people discover how to integrate their inner understanding with their outer expression and start to make a real difference in the world by simply being fully who they find themselves to be, individually and collectively? That kind of being is rare—not because it's complex, but because it's honest. And honesty in relationship can be revolutionary.

This chapter explores what might be stirring in these fragile experiments of togetherness. Not answers. Not movements. Just invitations—openings into the possible. A "what if…" space where imagination, vulnerability, and participation meet.

The Field as Invitation

Our group has never relied on charismatic figureheads or ideological frameworks—although in the early days, the guardianship of one of us with a profound intuitive sense of the field's potential did provide a vital orientation during times of uncertainty… and still, at times, will take us ever deeper into where we were venturing, peeling back layers some of us hadn't yet seen.

This kind of intuitive anchoring may be vital in the early stages—to help stabilise and protect the emerging field and can help deepen the transmission we experience together as the group continues to evolve.

Once the responsibility for the group's integrity begins to be shared by more of us, we discover that its real power lies in something quieter, more integrated, more connected:

in shared stillness,
in humble, discovered self-authority,
in the courage to meet without masks.

And strangely, this has made it deeply attractive.

Newcomers often arrive and feel immediately met. Not taught, not impressed—but seen.

Could it be that this resonance is itself a form of transmission? A new way of awakening—arising not from instruction, but from immersion in a shared field that opens inner space as a reflection of outer presence?

Witnessing Transformation

In one of our recent meetings, we found ourselves looking back to the early days—when it was just a few of us meeting. We remembered how at times, people would arrive full of doubt. Doubt about their own understanding. Doubt about whether their liberation was even possible.

Those early gatherings weren't always easy. Some of us were only just beginning to trust the truth we were starting to stand in. And when someone brought their doubt into the space, it could feel like it filled the room—sometimes with an energy that said, *this is valid, and I'm putting it out here whether you like it or not.* It carried weight. And that weight could muddy the clarity that was just starting to show itself between us.

What we began to discover—often by trial and error—was that the way through wasn't to argue or push back. It was for someone to speak from a place of *doubtlessness.* Not certainty. Not superiority. Just the quiet confidence that comes when you're rooted in something real. When someone did that, it changed the quality of the whole space. It deepened. It became stiller. More alive and more responsive.

There's something generous in being willing to speak from that vulnerable place. It doesn't come with guarantees or certainties. But when someone does it, it gives others permission—not to copy, but to trust themselves a little more.

Saying something out loud—naming what's real in you—can feel like a turning point. Like drawing a line and saying, "*I know this much. I can stand here.*" Someone in the group called it "*learning to trust that which is never-not-there.*" That line has stayed with us.

And the thing is, when you speak it and someone hears you—really hears you—it starts to land somewhere deeper in both you and the others in the group. You begin to live it—not just within the safety of the group, but in the wider world, where it truly asks something of you. That's when things start to shift. That's when this becomes more than just a special space—it starts to change how you show up in life.

We've watched it happen. Over and over again. Sometimes gradually. Sometimes all at once. But unmistakably. Like watching something open that can't be closed again.

A New Template of Being

One of the quiet but profound aspects of our group has been the way it allows us to explore new ways of being—together—beyond the inherited scripts of our cultures, communities, and even spiritual histories. In a time when gender relations are increasingly polarised, combative, or weaponised, we've stumbled into something far simpler and more healing: mutual presence.

At a recent meeting, one of the women spoke movingly about how deeply healing it was to sit in the presence of the men in the group—men who are spacious, integrated, and not needing to control or dominate. For her, as someone who has spent a lifetime advocating for women subjected to violence, simply feeling safe, open, and at ease in the company of men she did not know well was extraordinary. It marked the emergence of something longed-for but rarely witnessed: trust.

The impact of this didn't fully land during the meeting, though we recognised how significant it was for the person expressing it. It was only later—hours after the call had ended—that one of the group founders shared her recognition that something subtle but crucial had shifted.

She wrote an email to the group speaking of seeing the men not just as individuals, but as a collective presence—stable, generous, and quietly radiant. And the women, too, were expressing a collective wisdom, dignity, and courage in the group context.

This feels like a rich territory to explore further in future meetings. What we may be uncovering is not just interpersonal healing, but a relational intelligence that transcends the cultural battles and ancient wounds of gender altogether, offering a glimpse of how things could be between men and women, if enough care and presence are brought to the space between us.

Ethics Beyond the Self

One morning, following the meeting described above, a shift occurred that I hadn't anticipated. While reflecting on a personal ethical choice, I realised I could no longer make it in isolation. The relational field cultivated through our group had quietly restructured my sense of self. Or perhaps more accurately: I had opened myself to that restructuring—inviting the Unknown to shape me through the field's embrace.

My moral sense of 'me' now included the presence of others—not in a dissolving sense of oneness, but as a subtle binding through care and shared presence, a transpersonal inclusion. Integrity, once a solitary pursuit, had become relational. I found myself choosing from a wider place, knowing that each act could strengthen—or strain—the bond that unites us. PM

Cultural Evolution in Real Time

The group is more than a private circle of spiritual friends. Over time, it's become clear that something is not just shifting within us, or even between us—but through us. What we're participating in may be a form of real-time cultural evolution. A subtle rewiring of the collective nervous system. A new form of relational intelligence.

At times, it feels as if the space between us is growing its own awareness—or perhaps more accurately, supporting an awareness that transcends any one individual. An intelligence that arises from the deeper layers of the whole, where our commonality is connection, not difference. We're not just passive recipients of some external wisdom but both the source and ground of our own transformation.

We are not just developing better relational habits or becoming more sensitive communicators. We are witnessing the emergence of a new kind of coherence—one that may be reaching into and reshaping the foundational structures of how humans relate, belong, and become together.

This isn't unprecedented. The early Quaker meetings also gave rise to something larger than their own gatherings. In their stillness, a moral and social clarity emerged that went on to ripple outward—into abolition, peace movements, and education reform. Not through ideology, but through integrity—the kind that grows silently in the ground of shared presence.

What we're seeing now may be a new expression of that same impulse—one that belongs to this fragmented, digitised age, yet carries something timeless. What's evolving between us feels less like a method or philosophy, and more like a cultural mutation: an updated relational code embedded not in systems, but in felt experience. A new way of knowing ourselves in connection.

If that's true, it may not spread through teaching or effort. It may move like all true culture does—quietly, virally, through example. It doesn't demand to be understood. It just begins to shift what feels possible.

The Relational Lineage

Maybe awakening is no longer a solitary journey or a personal enlightenment—but a collective remembering. A lineage not passed down through bloodlines or succession but carried in the quality of our relating.

There is a thread that flows through all our meetings—unbroken, unmistakable. Each gathering feels connected to the very first, as though we are part of a continuous unfolding. What we're carrying together isn't static—it's alive, and it's evolving. And in some way, it seems to be carrying us, too.

The fire we've kindled doesn't just spread outward by adding new people or forming new groups. It deepens inward—into the collective psyche—where boundaries become places of exchange, not defence. Something subtle is being passed along, not through teaching, but through presence.

This isn't happening through evangelism or persuasion. Just as heat radiates naturally, something quiet seems to ripple outward from this space in all directions. A coherence. A field. A signal that something new—and ancient—is stirring.

We don't know how this will evolve or where it may lead. But its signature is already clear: trust, vitality, and deep receptivity. And it seems to be gathering strength, not through effort, but through constancy—through showing up, again and again, and letting the thread reveal itself.

Perhaps this isn't a discovery of something new, but an uncovering of what has always been present—just beneath the surface of the collective unconscious, waiting for the right relational conditions to become visible.

Could others pick up the thread and create their own gatherings—not as followers, but as co-creators? Not by imitation, but by attuning to the same underlying current in their own way?

The longing for truth, for real connection, is everywhere. What's arising between us may be part of a larger evolutionary wave—beyond dogma, beyond identity, beyond hierarchy. Not something invented, but something elemental—finally becoming available to those ready to carry it forward, with care.

Reflection:

In a world that increasingly demands certainty, outrage, and tribal loyalty—what does it mean to sit in open, undefended presence with others?

> Think of the relationships in your life where you feel most free, most alive. What if those moments weren't just personal, but part of something larger?

> What would change if you began to treat those spaces not just as pleasant coincidences, but as doorways into a deeper way of being together?

Motif 9:
The Future of Interbeing –

A Fractal Emergence

"The next Buddha may take the form of a community—a community practicing understanding and loving-kindness, a community practicing mindful living"

— Thich Nhat Hanh

ALCHEMY

Meditation: so many things to so many people
in the spiritual marketplaces of our time.

Clothed in Mind, Body, Spirit tropes
and touted as a path to a peaceful, gentle life,
it has the fragrance of escape about it.

It is so much more than that!
Discovering the innate stillness behind all
is merely a portal to a different dimension.

Sit with the silence.
Bask in the stillness.
Sink deeper and deeper.
Don't pause and rest
thinking you've arrived.

If you've truly 'let go' of control, you'll keep sinking—
beyond the realm of stillness—into a creative
maelstrom bubbling away:
a cauldron of infinite potential—
quantum fluctuations in the heart of nothingness.

Closer to the source, swim in this ocean of possibilities
and open yourself to its energies.
The creative impulse will accept your invitation.
In this alchemical laboratory you are a willing
participant,
a test model for what might emerge next.......

Dive into this space with others
and who knows what might be unleashed into the
world......

Glimpsing the Possible

This chapter begins not with a declaration, but with a question.

What if everything we've discovered so far is still just the beginning?

> Could it be that what we've stumbled upon—this humble, shared field of presence—is not just for us, but points to a new cultural potential?

Is what's happening between us a prototype—a seed of something that wants to grow?

Early Intimations of Future Possibilities

Just a few months after the group first came together, we were already exploring the possibility that we were strands in a larger evolutionary movement. In December 2022, one member shared this reflection in our chat space:

> *'The next Buddha will be the Sangha' Thich Nhat Hanh*
>
> *"I have been sceptical of this concept in the past, failing to see how such a sangha could avoid the politicking, corruption and power grabs that seem to beset even the best-intentioned communities and thereby ruining any hope of a transformative, elevated, sustainable, communal teaching model.*

There has recently been a revolution in my thinking however that has opened my mind to this as not only a possibility (and a wildly successful one), but also a potentially inevitable one.

This new teaching model depends at a foundational level on the selfless service and individual/collective 'enlightened mind' of the group. Up until now there has been little evidence that such an individual/collective/selfless 'enlightened mind' existed/was sustainable, but I believe that is no longer the case, and that we are now experiencing the beginnings of a new and much-needed leap in the evolution of spiritual instruction/transmission.

There are individual points of light across the globe these days: people awake to themselves and their own nature, who are not necessarily teachers but who feel the call to share their understandings and realizations with others.

These same individuals are often disenchanted with the state of the current spiritual environment/marketplace and the long-problematic teacher-student relationship and are looking for new ways to express the timeless wisdom and come together with others doing the same.

I believe these people are slowly starting to find each other and beginning to form the basis of such an international 'enlightened mind' community. When this international community establishes itself (not as a fixed entity/organization, but as naturally expressed 'structures' of this new evolutionary development), it will organically attract seekers and inquirers drawn to and ready to participate and become creative partners in this new entity." AS

The Scaling Paradox

Could the simplicity of what we're doing—listening deeply, being present, letting go of control—become the seed of something far larger?

The moment we ask, "Can this scale?" the field can vanish. It resists being turned into a method.

> But what if growth doesn't mean replication?
> What if it means resonance?

Not one big movement, but many small fires—each unique, each self-sustaining, yet sharing a common flame.

Organic Transmission

Rather than spreading through teaching, maybe the field spreads through presence.

Perhaps those who have deeply attuned to it become quiet carriers—people who don't need to explain it but embody it. As they meet others with similar longings, new groups might form—not by design, but by convergence.

The impulse is not to franchise a brand of awakening, but to follow the life that wants to keep flowing. Like mycelium under the soil, new pods might arise wherever the conditions are right.

Each new group could be entirely unique—shaped by those individuals present yet humming with the same underlying tone.

The Fabric of Trust

Could trust be the true infrastructure of shared awakening?

Not just trust in each other, but in the shared field itself—its timing, its intelligence, its gentle invitation to deepen.

Like threads interwoven, trust creates both strength and flexibility in our connections.

Without trust, we fall into rigid structures. With it, we find coherence without control—a pattern that emerges naturally from our collective presence.

We are weaving a tapestry in time and trust is both the warp and the weft of our collective experience, both as subtle structure holding us and opening up space for the unknown to shine through.

From Green Shoots to Coherent Systems

The question of scale is delicate. More people mean more possibility—but also more complexity, more projection, more entropy. Yet as we observe this emerging field, we're noticing patterns that suggest how coherence might naturally scale

> Those grounded in their own inner knowing appear to carry and hold the field.
>
> Those newly encountering the field seem drawn in by the atmosphere rather than explanation.
>
> The presence of trust appears to create conditions where truth emerges naturally.
>
> When someone slips into old patterns of defence, the field seems to respond rather than collapse.

This isn't control. It's a form of relational intelligence we're becoming familiar with. Like a murmuration of starlings, it moves as one, without central command. These initial observations invite us to look deeper into how such coherence functions.

The Group as a Living Portal

In Buddhist traditions, there is the idea of co-emergence—that nothing arises alone, but always in relation.

Perhaps these groups are not just gatherings, but portals: relational gateways through which something vaster can arrive. Something already here, waiting to be made visible through us.

The mystery is vast. The intelligence feels real.

We are not puppets—but we are not separate either. The group's unfolding has never felt like a linear plan. It has felt like a dance—one step appearing only when we take the last one.

We are not alone in this.

Evolution Through Us

Spiral Dynamics and Integral Theory suggest that consciousness evolves through stages—bouncing between the poles of autonomy and belonging until something deeper emerges.

Could it be that interbeing is that deeper thing? Not a compromise between the two, but a transcendence and a re-integration, into a deeper shared reality we rarely, if ever touch. A living coherence where difference isn't erased but honoured—becoming the very vehicle for intimacy

Interpersonal Awakening and the Wider Web – Practical Constraints

Let's be clear. We're not attempting to scale. There is no growth plan. We're simply following a natural, organic emergence within our group—one that seems to want to include more people under its umbrella. However, expansion brings other considerations into play.

A well-known principle in organisational theory suggests that as systems—like companies or communities—grow beyond a certain size, their internal complexity begins to inhibit their original agility. What once thrived on intimacy, coherence, and responsiveness can become sluggish or self-protective.

Dunbar's number proposes that around 150 people is the optimal size for a group to function with meaningful connection. Whether that holds for a group meeting within a shared virtual space via a screen interface is another question. How small would our 'windows' need to be to fit on a single display and maintain a sense of one community.

At this threshold, instead of scaling up into a single, ever-larger structure, it may be wiser to branch into smaller, semi-autonomous units—each retaining the original spirit while remaining agile and alive. Like cells dividing in a living organism, vitality is preserved not through expansion alone, but through intelligent, fractal replication.

Resonant Ignition

If, and when that time comes, we may need to learn from models already in operation—tapping into their hard-won insights. Dee Hock's concept of chaordic organisations, which honour the creative tension between coherence and chaos, offers one such example. These models don't impose structure but allow structure to emerge from the living dynamic between purpose and freedom.

But perhaps the most vital element in this emergence is what we might call "resonant ignition"—the mysterious process by which the quality of presence in one group catalyses similar qualities in another. This isn't about teaching methods or transferring knowledge. It's about transmission of a field of being.

Maybe as new groups emerge, one or two of us from the original group can spend time with them as they begin to establish themselves—a bit like carrying the original spark across to a new fire. But even this metaphor may be too linear. What if it is more akin to quantum entanglement—where connection happens instantaneously across distance, defying our conventional understanding of causality.

The Mechanisms of Resonance

Looking more deeply into the patterns that seem to lie behind coherent transmission, this resonance appears to operate through several distinct channels:

First, there's the direct experience of the field itself. When someone new enters our space and feels the quality of presence, something core within them recognizes it—not intellectually, but viscerally. It's as if a tuning fork within them begins to vibrate at the same frequency.

This recognition can happen in an instant and requires no explanation.

Second, there's the witnessing of authentic relationship. Seeing others relate from presence rather than persona creates a template that invites and welcomes similar authenticity. This is supported by validation when someone takes the risk to speak with vulnerability and the group responds positively. The field becomes visible not through description but through demonstration—through the living example of people meeting beyond their conditioning.

And maybe there is a third channel: what we might call "emergent coherence"—the way that a group that has experienced deep presence together develops a kind of shared attunement that makes it easier to drop into that state again, and easier for newcomers to sense and join that coherence. The relational field between people is supporting a kind of coherent pattern, both reliant on and also independent of the group members, that strengthens over time and invites others into its rhythm.

These mechanisms of resonance suggest that the spread of interbeing follows very different patterns than traditional movements or organizations. Rather than growing through recruitment or persuasion, it may spread through recognition and remembrance—awakening what is already latent in those it touches.

This deeper understanding shows us that while the process isn't passive it operates through principles quite different from conventional growth models. Resonant ignition requires intention and care. It asks us to tend the quality of our own presence, to create conditions where others can access their own depth, and to trust the intelligence of the field itself to guide the unfolding.

What makes this approach revolutionary is its inherent resistance to the pitfalls that have plagued spiritual and social movements throughout history: the tendency toward hierarchy, dogma, and the calcification of living insight into rigid doctrine. When transmission happens through resonance rather than instruction, these dangers naturally diminish.

The question then becomes not "How do we scale this?" but "How do we remain true to the quality that wants to spread of its own accord?" How do we stay attuned to the subtle intelligence that seems to be orchestrating this emergence from within?

The Ground Beneath the Meeting

On a practical note: our gatherings are sustained by a quieter kind of presence—the care taken to coordinate times, manage invitations, and navigate time zones. This backstage work often falls to just one or two of us, quietly tending to the rhythm that allows the deeper space to unfold. It ticks away in the background, and it really matters.

Even the most luminous meetings rest on these quiet, unglamorous acts of care—reminding us that even presence needs scaffolding.

And Perhaps that's the Real Invitation.

Not to scale, control, or replicate, but to stay true to what is alive—to listen deeply, respond authentically, and allow new expressions to emerge where the conditions are ripe. What began between a few of us is not ours to hold, but ours to honour.

It will find its way—not through force or formula, but through the quiet fidelity of those willing to meet, again and again, in the open space between us, and be prepared to discover and then live from deeper aspects of themselves in the process.

And if something in these pages resonates—if these words have pointed to something you feel a pull to engage with—if you too have glimpsed this subtle shift in the human field—consider this your invitation.

The next stage of our evolution won't arrive through systems or saviours, but through each of us, meeting with presence, humility, and care, wherever we are. The space is already opening.

Reflection:

> What if the space you long for is not elsewhere, but waiting to be born between you and another?

> What if you became the kindling? Who might you meet in presence today—and what might emerge between you?

You don't need to figure it out.

Just stay curious.

Stay open.

And follow the quiet pull of what wants to bloom.

Could it be that…….

In this digital age, perhaps awakening no longer wears robes and sits on mountaintops, but flickers between keystrokes and across oceans of digital space.

Maybe this, too, is the dance of Indra's Net—luminous nodes of awareness reflecting each other across time, distance, and form.

What we've discovered in our virtual gatherings challenges any assumption that digital connection must be shallow or disembodied. Instead, we've found that screens can become windows—portals through which authentic presence flows with surprising immediacy.

The technology itself is neither barrier nor enabler; it's simply the medium through which our intention travels. When that intention is presence, the digital space transforms from mere utility to sacred vessel.

Could it be that the global web of connection we've built—this nervous system of humanity spanning continents and cultures—is not just infrastructure but evolutionary architecture? Not just a tool for commerce and distraction, but a nascent capacity for collective consciousness?

In that sense, our group's journey—and this book—may not simply be documenting something new. They might be that something new.

A living expression of Gaia's mind, broadcasting through

the world wide web, and nestled within the Universal mind, finding its voice through unexpected channels.

As we transition from exploring possibilities to living them, perhaps the most profound realization is that the future we glimpse is not distant or theoretical. It's already here, emerging through each authentic connection, each moment of shared presence.

The Coda that follows is not an ending but a threshold—an invitation to recognize that you, too, are part of this unfolding story. The space that remains between these words and your reading of them is where the real transmission happens. It's where the field continues to expand, reaching beyond the confines of our original group into the wider web of life that includes you.

KIND HEARTS

To be Awake
is not to simply swap identities—
from a 'limited known'
to an 'unlimited unknown'.
Any fixed identity is a prison.

It is to be willing to live
with the intimate uncertainty
of having no idea who you are
in any single moment—
and being excited to discover it.

Life becomes an adventure,
a journey of fresh-eyed wonder—
a playful unfolding, dancing within limitation,
yet letting the limitless potential
of the universe flow through you.

You can be many things in one day,
morphing through multiple roles—
an Alec Guinness in Kind Hearts & Coronets—
each one held with the lightest touch,
and the deepest care, compassion, and attention.

Like a Swiss Army knife
with an infinitude of tools,
gently poised on the edge of the unknown,
ready to respond
to whatever life unleashes your way.

Coda

*"All shall be well, and all shall be well,
and all manner of thing shall be well"*

— Lady Julian of Norwich

The Space That Remains

I didn't set out to write a guidebook, or even to offer a vision. It was a visceral response to reading a history of Liberal thought and realising that it was missing the next chapter—the vision needed to take it to the next level.

And I realised through working within our group that this was what was unfolding between us. What has emerged in these pages is simply what we've lived—together. A record of something real, tender, and still in motion.

Over time, the group itself has become more than a place of exploration. Without roles or hierarchy, it has revealed a quiet capacity to teach—not through instruction, but through presence. The field we share seems to invite each person inward, toward a deeper intimacy with themselves and with life.

Rather than directing or shaping anyone's experience, the group holds a spaciousness where people begin to sense the field directly. They feel the openness, the gentle coherence, the absence of pressure—and something in them relaxes. Walls dissolve. Something softens. A subtle recognition arises: that it is safe to be here, to be real, in the company of others who are equally engaged in the mystery, and this builds a subtle confidence to drop the pretence and be their real selves.

And perhaps we are on the threshold of something more: When we attune ourselves to this field of universal being that contains and illumines everything, the potential for transformation extends beyond individual awakening to the very fabric of our relationships.

For, as we reach toward and open ourselves to this field of infinite possibilities—allowing it to claim more of us—we participate in illuminating and transforming the living connections between us. What emerges is not just transformed individuals but a transformed collective entity with its own integrity and intelligence. The men's group becomes more than the sum of individual men; the women's circle transcends its individual participants.

This shift from individual to relational transformation carries profound implications for how society might function—moving from structures built on separate selves pursuing separate interests to living systems of relationship that can hold complexity, diversity, and wholeness simultaneously. What we're glimpsing in these small groups may be the embryonic form of a fundamentally different social architecture.

This unspoken transmission—a resonance that opens rather than informs—is perhaps the truest teacher and architect of change. Through it we're witnessing the early stirrings of a new way of being human together—a different rhythm in the collective body.

Not a loud revolution of banners and pronouncements, but something quieter and more fundamental. A shift felt in the relational field itself—in how we meet, how we listen, how we dare to not-know together. Something so alive that it awakens us into the presence that is our birthright.

Over time, three currents have quietly made themselves known at the heart of this emergence:

>   —the unfolding of individual authenticity,
>   —the coherence of the relational field,
>   —and the emergence of a subtle intelligence that seems to guide from within.

These aren't theories, but patterns we've witnessed repeatedly—showing us that something deeper is possible when we meet each other in presence.

What if small gatherings like our group, scattered across the globe, are not isolated experiments but the early constellations of a new emergence? What if the future is already arriving—not through force or ideology, but through subtle synchrony, convergence and resonance?

It is certainly the time. Never has this approach been more needed, nor the moment more pressing.

This book is not a conclusion. It's a question in motion.

If it has stirred something in you—a quiet recognition, a sense of possibility, or a longing that won't go back to sleep—then perhaps you are already part of this unfolding.

The future we're glimpsing emerges in the space between us, one real encounter at a time.

Maybe this book is one of the sparks, flying away from the original fire, ready to start new fires wherever it lands...

Keep listening. Something beautiful is already beginning.

Harmonics of Meaning

A Glossary of Terms and Resonances

*"The total number of minds in the universe is one.
In fact, consciousness is a singularity
phasing within all beings"*

— Erwin Schrodinger

The Field

A subtle, living presence that reveals itself in the space between individuals when authenticity, stillness, and deep listening are shared. Not something external or magical, but one consciousness—always present—coming into view when we step out of the way. It carries a quiet intelligence, not separate from us, yet perceivable only when we no longer centre ourselves. The Field holds us, yet it is not made by us—it is the ground of our being, uncovered in relationship.

Presence

The quality of being fully here—attentive, undefended, and free of inner commentary. It is not something one performs, but a natural state that emerges when the mind quiets and connection deepens.

Awakening

Not a fixed state or goal, but an unfolding recognition of the ever-present reality beneath identity, thought and narrative. In this book, awakening is both personal and relational—something that happens within and between us.

Interbeing

Introduced by Buddhist philosopher *Thich Nhat Hanh*, this term refers to the reality that nothing exists independently. Everything co-arises in relation. Here, it also implies a way of relating honouring both the individual and the shared space between.

Authenticity

The felt sense of speaking, acting, and responding from your real self—not from a role, expectation, or performance. It is not about raw emotional exposure, but the deeper simplicity of being true in the moment. It has a quality of freshness and revelation, rather than speaking from known concepts.

Intersubjective Coherence

A phrase pointing to the alignment and clarity that emerges when individuals come into resonance together—not by agreement, but by attuning to a shared deeper knowing. It's when something greater than the sum of its parts comes into view, as a common perspective emerging between, not held by one.

Relational Intelligence

An evolving capacity to listen, speak, and sense into the space between people with attunement and care. It includes knowing when to step in, when to yield, and when to let silence speak.

Convergent Evolution

The independent emergence of similar traits or innovations in different systems under similar conditions. It suggests that certain breakthroughs—biological, cultural, or spiritual—may be part of a deeper, shared pattern of development.

The Space Between

More than metaphor, this refers to the dynamic, sacred "third space" that emerges when two or more people meet in presence. It is not neutral territory—it's alive, responsive, and full of possibility.

Resonant Ignition

A moment when the shared field of presence becomes so attuned that it sparks a deep inner recognition or awakening in another, leaping across separation without instruction.

Original Face

A Zen-inspired phrase pointing to the unconditioned self before identity, before story. In the context of the group, it signals the recognition of each other as that ungraspable essence—pure, awake, and unrepeatably unique, yet with no edges or boundaries between.

Thanatos

The archetypal energy of the ego's death-grip—contractive, self-protective, and willing to sacrifice the whole to preserve its image or control.

Eros

The life-affirming force that draws us into connection, creativity, and shared becoming—an expansive impulse toward collective coherence.

Field Notes & Jazz Variations

Appendices

*"No man is an island, entire of itself;
every man is a piece of the continent,
a part of the main…"*

— John Donne, Meditation XVII

Before entering the appendices, let us pause and widen the lens. This ancient image from the Avatamsaka Sutra evokes the mystery and intimacy of interconnectedness—each of us both whole in ourselves and wholly woven into the All.

INDRA'S NET

A precious jewel lies at the centre
of each node in the net of Indra.
Each jewel reflects all others,
intimately connected to each and every one

Each jewel is a locus of Being.
Most are only truly aware of themselves
as self-contained, autonomous entities,
unaware of the vast, infinite, multidimensional
network they are part of—
interconnected, interdependent, alive.

As each locus of Being awakens to itself,
it begins to recognise its place in the whole.
The identity as a single, isolated node
is gradually subsumed into the entire net—
beyond any concept of limitation,
beyond any fixed sense of self—
yet still holding the specific vantage point
of its unique location in the weave.

Each of us, as a locus of Being,
is both the whole and the part:
the entire net and the particular jewel.
Both are absolutely true.
The unbroken integrity of the All
encompasses and embraces
the richness, diversity, and depth
of each facet—
weaving the infinite complexity of its parts
into a profoundly simple whole.

What follows now is not an ending, but an opening—fragments, patterns, and playful reflections that continue the weave. Like jazz, these variations riff on the central themes of this book, sometimes returning to familiar motifs, sometimes venturing into unexpected improvisations. Enjoy the unfolding...

Appendix I:
Glimpses from the Future: Invitations to a Wider Field

While this book has focused primarily on the emergence of shared presence within our group, the essence of interpersonal awakening we've discovered may have wider applications.

History shows us that contemplative communities often catalyse social change far beyond their original scope—the Quakers, for instance, whose silent meetings and commitment to "that of God in everyone" fuelled movements for abolition, women's rights, and prison reform.

In that spirit, we offer these glimpses into possibilities—not as prescriptions but as invitations held in an open palm, gifts from a future that beckons us forward into new ways of being:

1. Political Polarization

When people meet beyond their ideological identities, something shifts. The field creates a space where opposing viewpoints can be held not as threats but as different perspectives within a larger whole. Not to change minds, but to remember our shared humanity first—creating ground for genuine dialogue rather than debate.

2. Community Building

Local communities might discover that decisions made from shared presence have a different quality—less reactive, more attuned to the needs of all. Town halls and community gatherings could evolve from battlegrounds of competing interests to spaces where collective wisdom emerges.

3. Education

What if classrooms became fields of shared presence? Not just places of knowledge transfer, but environments where young people learn to listen deeply—to themselves, to each other, to the world. The emphasis shifts from accumulating information to cultivating the capacity for presence, curiosity, and authentic connection.

4. Organizational Culture

Businesses and organizations might find that meetings held in shared presence yield different results than those driven by agenda alone. Innovation emerges not from pressure but from the spaciousness that allows new patterns to form. Leadership becomes less about direction and more about tending the field where creativity and collaboration naturally arise.

5. Conflict Resolution

In settings of deep conflict, the field offers a third way beyond fight or flight. It creates space where opposing parties can be heard not just intellectually but felt in their humanity. Resolution emerges not through compromise but through a shift in the relational field itself.

Living the Shared Field

These are not programs to implement but possibilities and potentialities to explore—exciting new horizons that beckon us forward to engage in the world beyond our shared meditative-contemplative spaces. The approach is not to apply techniques but to embody presence—trusting that as the quality of our attention shifts, so too will the systems and structures we inhabit—presence rippling out from the common centre we share extending out beyond limits and quietly but insistently bringing constructive change in its wake.

The invitation is simple: bring the quality of presence you've discovered into these wider domains. Not as something separate from daily life, but as the very ground from which action emerges.

The results may surprise us all.

Appendix II: Resonant Echoes

While the shared awakening described in this book emerged organically within our group—without direct connection to any single tradition—it's clear we are not alone.

Across time and culture, many thinkers, mystics, and explorers have sensed a similar potential in the space between us.

What follows are a series of potent glimpses into this wider evolutionary landscape of intersubjective awakening—each expressed in its own unique voice.

They are not offered as signposts or summaries, but as resonant echoes—glimmers of the same mystery, seen from different vantage points, like the nodes on Indra's net.

If one of these echoes stirs something in you, may it deepen your own unfolding within the vast mystery we are exploring together.

Martin Buber – I and Thou

> *"When two people relate to each other authentically and humanly, God is the electricity that surges between them."*
>
> — Martin Buber

Quaker Practice – Silent Listening and Discernment

"In the silence, we do not merely wait for God to speak; we listen for the still, small voice that speaks within us and among us."

— Quaker Faith and Practice

David Bohm – Dialogue as Shared Meaning

"Suppose we were able to share meanings freely without a compulsive urge to impose our view or conform to those of others and without distortion and self-deception. Would this not constitute a real revolution in culture?"

— David Bohm

Otto Scharmer – 'Theory U' and the Art of Presencing

"When we attend to the silence within, we become aware of a deeper source of knowing—and begin to act from the emerging future rather than the patterns of the past."

— Otto Scharmer

Parker J. Palmer – 'Circles of Trust' and the Quiet Approach to Soul

"The soul is like a wild animal—tough, resilient, savvy, self-sufficient, and yet exceedingly shy. If we want to see a wild animal, the last thing we should do is go crashing through the woods... Instead, we might walk quietly into the woods, sit silently for an hour or two, and wait."

—Parker J. Palmer, A Hidden Wholeness

Thomas Hübl – Collective Trauma and the Mystical We

> *"Collective trauma is the residue of unintegrated experiences that are stored in the collective field. When we bring awareness and presence to these areas, healing and integration can occur, allowing for a deeper connection and emergence of collective wisdom."*
> — Thomas Hübl

Thomas Steininger & Elizabeth Debold – Emergent Dialogue and the Intersubjective Field

> *"The practice is one of speaking when spoken through; it aspires to let us connect to the intersubjective field or that which is bigger than us."*
> —Thomas Steininger, Emergent Dialogue

3rd Space

> *"Third Space is a field of presence where the deepest essence of who we are can be met, and where something beyond any individual can speak."*
> — Third Space

Jeff Carreira – Author & Teacher

> *"The deepest level of collective awakening is when the collective being awakens to its own existence—it is both dependent and independent of the individuals present."*
> —Jeff Carreira— from the talk Collective Awakening and the Art of Self Forgetting (YouTube, 2021)

Patricia Albere – Evolutionary Collective

"Belonging is a primary need... We need to embrace a new, higher order of belonging that includes the complexity of being profoundly unique and in communion with others within shared unity."

— Patricia Albere, Evolutionary Belonging

Geesje Stroo – Soul-Oriented Education

"Learning in Living Light invites you to a more universal perspective on our approach to education, one that acknowledges that we are all energetically connected within a larger cosmic field."

— Geesje Stroo.

Ken Wilber and Integral Theory – Evolution of Consciousness

"An integral vision draws together the subjective, the objective, the individual, and the collective dimensions of reality into a unified framework."

—Ken Wilber.

Jean Gebser – Structures of Consciousness

"The present is not a mere summation of the past, but the presence of origin."

— Jean Gebser, The Ever-Present Origin

Bernardo Kastrup – Analytic Idealism

"We are all dissociated alters of the same universal consciousness, dreaming up our lives in the same mind."

— Bernardo Kastrup

Spiral Dynamics – The Evolutionary Dance of Self and Group

> *"Man is not static. He is emerging. He is unfolding. His psychology is not a finished product sealed off in a test-tube. Rather, he is a rising and falling living system, a spiralling process, marked by progressive subordination of older, lower-order behaviour systems to newer, higher-order systems as man's existential problems change."*

— Clare W. Graves.

Echoes from the Sacred Past

Alongside the contemporary voices exploring this emergent intersubjective terrain, there are also resonances in the deep contemplative roots of the world's enduring wisdom traditions. While often obscured by dogma or institutional power, a quieter thread has persisted—mystics, poets, and prophets who have pointed to the same space of presence and unity we are discovering anew. What follows are a few such echoes—ancient, yet startlingly alive.

Richard Rohr – Communion as Shared Presence

> *"The divine indwelling is never an isolated reality. It is always discovered in mutuality and communion— where two or three are gathered in conscious love, there is the Presence."*

— The Divine Dance: The Trinity and Your Transformation

John O'Donohue – The Great Belonging

"Belonging does not merely shelter you from the sense of being separate and different; its more profound intention is the awakening of the Great Belonging which embraces everything. At the root of our hunger to belong therefore, is the desire to awaken this hidden affinity... we know we are not outsiders cut off from everything around us but rather participants at the very heart of creation."

— Eternal Echoes

Indra's Net – A Metaphor of Interbeing (Hindu/Buddhist)

"The Net of Indra is a profound and subtle metaphor for the structure of reality. Imagine a vast net; at each crossing point there is a jewel; each jewel is perfectly clear and reflects all the other jewels in the net... The jewel in this metaphor stands for an individual being, or an individual consciousness... Every jewel reflects every other jewel in the net, and every reflected image also reflects every other jewel."

— Indra's Net

Rumi – The Community of the Spirit

"There is a community of the spirit. Join it, and feel the delight of walking in the noisy street and being the noise."

— Rumi, The Essential Rumi, trans. Coleman Barks

Llewellyn Vaughan-Lee – Sufi Mysticism

"Our heart knows what our mind has forgotten—it knows the sacred that is within all that exists, and through a depth of feeling we can once again experience this connection, this belonging."
— Llewellyn Vaughan-Lee, The Return of the Feminine and the World Soul

Thich Nhat Hanh – Buddhist Interbeing

"The next Buddha may take the form of a community—a community practicing understanding and loving-kindness, a community practicing mindful living. This may be the most important thing for Earth's survival."
— Thich Nhat Hanh

Sri Aurobindo – Integral Yoga

"The Divine is not only in us but in all: to see and feel Him in all is the true and wide basis of community and the condition of a divine society."
— Sri Aurobindo, The Synthesis of Yoga

Rabbi Arthur Green – Jewish Mysticism

"Religion is not about the individual soul standing alone before God. It is about building community, creating sacred space and sacred time together, and allowing our lives to be transformed by that shared context."
— Arthur Green, Radical Judaism

Threads

These voices, from many paths and places, all point toward something alive in the space between us. Let them speak in their own way.

If one tugs at you, feel free to pull on the thread and see where it takes you.

The invitation is always the same: to stay open, to meet others beyond assumption, and to listen deeply to what is longing to emerge—together.

Appendix III:
Living Patterns – Metaphors for the Field in Motion

What if the field between us has its own ways of growing?

Not like a blueprint or curriculum, but more like a forest, a tide, a symphony—always in motion, always improvising.

This appendix is not an exploration of theories, but a playful constellation of patterns that might mirror how shared presence evolves over time.

If you've ever been part of a living, breathing group presence, you may have sensed that it doesn't evolve in a straight line. It moves as life does—in rhythms, pulses, spirals, and sudden leaps.

This appendix offers a handful of metaphors—Some come from nature's wisdom, some from philosophical models of consciousness, and others from living systems and cultural evolution. Each represents a way that coherence can arise without being imposed—when trust, presence, and connection become the soil for something new.

We don't know how this unfolding will continue. But these models offer glimpses—like seeds scattered across time—of how complexity can give rise to harmony, and how something new might take root.

Patterns in Nature

Nature doesn't grow in straight lines. It unfolds through spirals, pulses, tides, and networks—always adapting, always alive.

These patterns don't explain the field, but they might reflect something of its rhythm.

The Fibonacci Spiral – Natural Expansion

In the Fibonacci sequence, each new number arises from the sum of the two before it. Growth builds upon what's already alive. So too with this shared field—each deepening, each new member, each insight grows out of what has come before.

Over time, this unfolding tends toward a golden ratio—a harmony that isn't imposed, but discovered.

And like in nature, not everything survives. Some things fall away and feed the roots. Even decay has its place in the spiral.

The field evolves like a plant—spiralling outward in dynamic balance.

Lunar Tides – Phases of Intensity

Like the moon and the sea, the field breathes.

Some meetings feel electric—alive with revelation and resonance. Others feel quiet, inward, consolidating what's been touched. Neither state is better. Both are necessary.

Trying to force constant expansion burns out the roots. Listening to the tide, we learn to honour rhythm, not rush.

Learning to honour the rhythm is part of the awakening.

Rhizomes – Networks Without a Centre

Mushrooms spread underground through a vast, hidden network of connection. Bamboo sends out shoots laterally, not upward.

This is how our group has grown—not top-down, but sideways.

No one has planned or directed it.

New nodes emerge where conditions are right.

Awakening no longer needs a guru. It can spread through contact, coherence, and trust in the unknown.

Maps of Meaning

Some explorers of consciousness and culture have tried to chart the territory—tracing the arcs of human development, consciousness, and complexity.

These maps don't capture the field, but they offer clues, glimpses, and language for things we've only just begun to touch.

They're not instructions—just invitations to see from a wider view.

Spiral Dynamics—Growth through Complexity

This model suggests that human values evolve in spirals—oscillating between autonomy (freedom, individuality) and belonging (safety, shared identity).

With time, a higher-order synthesis can emerge: not by resolving the tension, but by integrating and transcending it.

It's not a hierarchy, but a dance—a movement toward deeper inclusion and fluid coherence.

Integral Theory—Growing in All Directions

Ken Wilber's model invites us to see reality through four lenses: inner and outer, individual and collective.

True growth, he suggests, unfolds across all these dimensions—not just in personal insight, but in how we relate, create, and co-evolve.

The shared interior—the "We" space—may be the next frontier of awakening.

Organisational Theory—Fractal Forms and Living Limits

As groups grow, complexity can dilute coherence. Some models suggest growth isn't about getting bigger, but about replicating the core essence in smaller, self-organising units.

Dee Hock's idea of "chaordic" organisations—balancing chaos and order—echoes a natural way forward: growth through resonance, not control.

In this view, shared awakening spreads not through scale, but through coherence—each node alive, responsive, and true to the whole.

Information Theory – The Universe as Pattern

Some scientists now suggest that the fabric of reality may be woven from information itself—not just particles or energy, but subtle codes of probability, pattern, and meaning.

It's a view that echoes mystical traditions: consciousness as the ground of being, with each mind a receiver tuned into a shared field.

In that light, the coherence we sense between us may be more than metaphor.

It might be how a deeper intelligence shows itself through resonance, wherever openness allows.

Forces in Motion

Some models point not to structure, but to movement—dynamic energies that shape how growth unfolds. These ideas explore the subtle forces, rhythms, and impulses that animate change from within.

The Three Gunas—A Dynamic Balance

In Indian philosophy, all of nature is shaped by three interwoven forces: sattva (clarity and spaciousness), rajas (movement and momentum), and tamas (grounding and stability).

Each one plays a role in the unfolding of life.

These qualities feel familiar in group process. At times there is forward motion, at other times stillness, and sometimes a sense of consolidation or resting.

Their interplay may offer a way of understanding the field's rhythm—not as fixed states, but as energies in continuous relationship.

Patricia Albere – Evolutionary Collective

Working at the edge where spirituality becomes intersubjective, Patricia Albere articulates the intensity and transformative potential of relational presence. Her work invites full-bodied, full-hearted engagement—not as a performance, but as a path of purification and collective emergence.

"It's about engagement. It's about full-out showing up and engaging and allowing that full-out engagement to start to purify and dissolve the separation."

Autopoiesis—The Art of Staying Alive

Borrowed from systems theory, autopoiesis describes how living systems maintain themselves through internal coherence, not external control.

Like a flock adjusting mid-flight, they sense, respond, reshape. What keeps them whole isn't structure—it's sensitivity.

The group doesn't evolve by adding parts, but by reorganizing itself in response to what arises. Identity comes not from rules, but from shared values—like presence, listening, humility.

Self-renewing, self-sensing.

The field is a 'becoming' not a 'thing'.

The Evolutionary Impulse—When the Cosmos Gets Personal

Some suggest evolution isn't just random mutation, but an unfolding intelligence—subtle, persistent, creative.

Maybe the field that emerged in our group wasn't created but discovered.

Maybe it was ready. Maybe it had always been here—waiting.

Waiting for enough of us to become quiet enough, coherent enough, receptive enough…

to carry it forward.

Maybe the universe wasn't just nudging us—maybe it was waiting for us to become vehicles for its next unfolding.

Or maybe… this is what it feels like when evolution becomes aware of itself.

The Playful Truth

All of the above is possibility, not prescription—metaphor, not mechanism.

None of it is needed to follow where the field of being you've encountered in these pages might lead.

But if something here makes you smile or sparks a flicker of curiosity—welcome.

Trust the unfolding.

Appendix IV: Distilled Wisdom from the Group Field

"Wisdom unveils itself in Presence."

The following six qualities revealed themselves in the writing of this book—almost an accidental uncovering of the catalysts that support the emergence and resilience of the field between us.

They are not teachings, doctrines, or claims. They are fragments of clarity, glimpses of essence—hints at the personal journey each of us must undertake to carry the field forward, almost as guardians of the flame.

They arose not from any one voice, but from the space between us.

Trust
—to accept your experience as it is, without flinching.

Courage
—to keep showing up when times get tough.

Humility
—to recognise our failings and still drop our defences.

Honesty
—to face what is uncomfortable and take full responsibility for our part.

Compassion

—to have faith in our deepest intention and follow the quiet call of integrity.

Engagement

—to step in fully without holding back. *Presence* arises when we are wholly present.

DON'T WAIT

Don't wait.

Don't wait for any experience
to confirm who you already are.
You are beyond any and every experience.

Don't doubt—
that only tempts you to await confirmation.

You are already prior to everything,
embodying the ungraspable mystery
at the heart of Being.

This mystery only known
in each moment,
by being itself—
ever untouched
by the grasping, defining mind.

Don't wait—
to share this with others.
The mystery is not yours alone.
It reveals itself
where presence meets presence—
in the silent space between.

A Last Echo

"The void is not silent. I have always thought of it more and more as a transitional space, an in-between space. It's very much to do with time. I have always been interested as an artist in how one can somehow look again for the very first moment of creativity where everything is possible and nothing has actually happened. It's a space of becoming..."

— Anish Kapoor, reflecting on his 1998 retrospective exhibition at the Hayward Gallery, London Southbank

Acknowledgements

Firstly, a big warm thank you to Anne, Margaret and Harry—the other "three of four" originals—for their friendship, guidance and Love, and for sharing the nurturing of the spark. To have such companions on the way is a gift and a joy.

Thank you to the many faces who have passed through the portals of the group, some becoming regulars, some occasional visitors and some who felt their particular path led off in different directions. I celebrate the heart connection that we meet in.

Thank you to those in the group who offered their own insights into engaging in the shared field: Anne, Margaret, Albert, Wren, JP, Jared and Anne Michaud. Your words carry your own personal authority yet resonate with the essence of the field.

And a very grateful thank you to the readers of the evolving text and its many iterations. Your insights, suggestions and reflections as to both content and tone have been invaluable and have helped to craft what feels like the combined work of the group expressed through my typing…..

One of the readers who offered feedback as the book neared completion was Anne Michaud—a newer member of the group. She is French-speaking from Quebec (with excellent English), and her reflections on the book opened up a rich inquiry into how language can both connect and obscure. She found the title *The Space Between Us* somewhat misleading. From her perspective, there is no space, no boundary—we are the space we meet in. She shared that French feels more relational and expressive to her, whereas English can carry a more transactional, subject-object tone. When she translated the title into French, it became *Ce qui nous relie*—"that which connects us."

Her insight stayed with me. And yet, I chose not to change the title. *The Space Between Us* emerged early on as the central motif around which the book began to cohere—it held the tension, the inquiry, the paradox at the heart of these explorations. In English, the phrase carries a kind of ambiguity: it can imply a gap, a separation, but it also gestures toward the very medium of connection. This book lives inside that ambiguity—the illusion of distance, the truth of connection, and the spacious awareness that holds both.

Thank you to Ian Dunt, whose book 'How to be a Liberal' planted the seeds for this book. His history of liberal thought—origins, challenges and pitfalls—opened my eyes to how precious a gift this field of inter-being is and how it might be the next step to help break through the cultural, social and political impasse of this first quarter of the 21st Century.

I wrote him a very naïve letter after reading the first few chapters of his book and this book is my response to cover my embarrassment. I do hope he gets to read it and maybe we can start a conversation.......

And finally a big hug to Rade….. just because it feels right.

About the Author

Peter has walked an unconventional path, weaving together diverse roles—optometrist, artist and life model, Santa Claus, and a spiritual seeker—into an illuminating journey of awakening beyond identity. A chance encounter with Ganesh in 1993 at a liminal moment of his life, ignited a deep longing that led him through transformative highs and intense trials, including time with a controversial guru. Each experience, whether in stillness or struggle, stripped away another layer of the non-essential, revealing the deeper thread of presence running through it all. Now, through his blog 'Facets of the Diamond' and his engagement with an emergent field of shared awakening, he explores the meeting point of personal autonomy and collective transformation, inviting others into the unfolding mystery of presence.

"Facets of the Diamond" https://www.petermitchell.life/

Writings revealed in the silence of presence and shaped by lived experience—offered as poems, articles, and a book that traces a shared awakening.

Some of his Haiku can be found in "*Tranquility: An Anthology of Haiku*" edited by Gabriela Marie Milton and published by Literary Revelations.

Manufactured by Amazon.com.au
Sydney, New South Wales, Australia